CLOTHIERS

CLOTHIERS

by
Irene M. Franck
and
David M. Brownstone

A Volume in the
Work Throughout History Series

A Hudson Group Book

Facts On File Publications
New York, New York ● Oxford, England

CLOTHIERS

Library of Congress Cataloging-in-Publication Data
Franck, Irene M.
   Clothiers.
   (Work throughout history)
   Bibliography: p.
   Includes index.
   1. Clothing workers—History. 2. Clothing trade—
Job descriptions—History. I. Brownstone, David M.
II. Title. III. Series.
HD8039.C6F73 1986   687'.023'73   86-8927
ISBN O-8160-1442-6

Printed in the United States of America
10 9 8 7 6 5 4 3 2 1

Text Design by Debbie Glasserman
Composition by Facts On File/Maxwell Photographics

iv

Contents

Preface

Clothiers is a book in the multivolume series, *Work Throughout History*. Work shapes the lives of all human beings; yet surprisingly little has been written about the history of the many fascinating and diverse types of occupations men and women pursue. The books in the *Work Throughout History* series explore humanity's most interesting, important, and influential occupations. They explain how and why these occupations came into being in the major cultures of the world, how they evolved over the centuries, especially with changing technology, and how society's view of the occupation has changed. Throughout, we focus on what it was like to do a particular kind of work—for example, to be a farmer, glassblower, midwife, banker, building contractor, actor, astrologer, or weaver—in centuries past and right up to today.

Because many occupations have been closely related to one another, we have included at the end of each article references to other overlapping occupations. In preparing this series, we have drawn on a wide range of general works on social, economic, and occupational history, including many on everyday life throughout history. We consulted far too many such wide-ranging works to list them all here; but at the end of each volume is a list of suggestions for further reading, should readers want to learn more about any of the occupations included in the volume.

Many researchers and writers worked on the preparation of this series. For *Clothiers*, the primary researcher-writers were Joan Naper and Thomas Crippen. Our thanks go to them for their fine work; to our expert typists, Shirley Fenn, Nancy Fishelberg, and Mary Racette; to our most helpful editors at Facts On File, first Kate Kelly and then James Warren, and their assistant Claire Johnston; to our excellent developmental editor, Vicki Tyler; and to our publisher, Edward Knappman, who first suggested the *Work Throughout History* series and has given us gracious support during the long years of its preparation.

Irene M. Franck
David M. Brownstone

Introduction

The work of clothiers is all around us. The clothes we wear, the sheets and blankets we sleep under, the towels we dry with, the carpets we walk on, the curtains and drapes that decorate and shield our rooms, the tapestries that beautify our walls, the upholstery of the chairs we sit on—all these and more are examples of the clothiers' art and craft.

Fibers have been worked to form cloth since before 8000 B.C. Flax, from which linen is made, was commonly grown in early Europe and Egypt. Wool was a specialty of the early peoples of Mesopotamia in the Near East. India was long famed for its cotton, as the American South would be in modern times. And China excelled at making silk, keeping the secrets of silkmaking from the rest of the world for many centuries, perhaps for over 2,000 years.

The people who made all this possible, the ones who handled the all-important first steps in the clothmaking process, were the *fiber workers*. It was they who disentangled the flax and cotton fibers from the unwanted parts of the plant, then cleaned, washed, and smoothed it until it was ready to be spun into yarn. Wool and silk workers did much the same thing, except their fibers came from animals. The wool had to first be cut from living sheep, then carefully combed to smooth out the tangles. Silk was spun by the silkworm as an outer covering (as it prepared to transform itself into a moth) called a cocoon. Silk workers had to be extremely skilled at unwinding the fragile silk filaments without breaking them. Much of this work calls for such a delicate or expert touch that it is still, in this modern age of the machine, done by hand.

The next step in the clothmaking process was handled by the *spinners*. Using a spindle to hold the thread and a whorl to rotate the spindle, these specialists have for thousands of years turned raw fibers into yarn ready to be woven. That this work was traditionally—though not solely—done by women is indicated by the centuries-old term *spinster*, to refer to a woman who has never been married.

The next stage was handled by the *weavers*. Before the age of modern machines, it took four to six spinners to supply yarn for one weaver. Interworking two sets of threads—one horizontal and the other vertical—the weaver created cloth, the width of the fabric being limited by the width of the loom, the structure on which it was woven. Weavers create beautiful patterns on the cloth they weave by varying the colors of the threads they use. For thousands of years, skilled weavers have had high status among artisans, though with a change of fashion many could be thrown out of work and starve. In England just before the Industrial Revolution, for example, some weavers dressed and lived like gentlemen and ladies. But when machines took over many of the spinning and weaving processes, many were unable to make a living and the practice of fine hand-weaving declined dramatically.

From the weaver, cloth went to other specialists who would prepare the cloth for use; these were the *cloth finishers. Dyers* used animal and plant substances to give yarn a whole range of colors, sometimes before it was woven, but often after being woven. Dyers would work at very large vats, turning over the cloth so it would dye evenly. *Fullers* then took the cloth, cleaned it, and stretched it out on the tenterhooks to dry. Afterward, they would raise the nap, the fibers that stuck out from the woven surface. Finally, *shearers* clipped the nap with special scissors to leave the surface with the desired smooth, even texture.

Finished cloth was now ready to be used or worn. That included cloth meant for wearing, for in many parts of the world and for many centuries, clothing consisted simply of lengths of fabric wrapped or draped about the body. Only in northern Eurasia had fitted clothing become the norm before modern times. There, *tailors* and *dressmakers* gradually developed the specialty of sewing clothes for men and women. Generally, clothing was custom-made, that is, designed to fit the individual who ordered it. Only in the last century or so has ready-to-wear clothing been produced by *needleworkers* who never saw their customers. Today, much clothing is made by needleworkers in large factories, while the few tailors and dressmakers who still work on their own focus on repairs and alterations to clothing.

Working closely with dressmakers over the centuries were the *milliners*. Originally, milliners specialized in providing accessories of all kinds to complete a fashionable woman's costume. Only later did they specialize more particularly in making women's hats. Specialists in making men's hats were called *hatters*. Their work was quite separate from that of the milliners. Also, they often used different materials, such as straw or felt, which they made from animal hairs stripped from skins.

Working with the skins themselves were the *shoemakers* and other *leatherworkers*. They had to go through their own preparation process. *Tanners* performed the very messy business of soaking and stripping the hides, then drying and stretching them for use. The prepared leather was then ready to be made into a variety of objects, not only shoes but also a whole range of items from belts and gloves to armor and briefcases. One group, the *furriers*, specialized in making clothing, hats, and other gear out of skins with the hair left on.

Because clothing and other items made of fabric are needed in every aspect of life, clothiers for much of history were found in every hamlet, or even in every house. But around the turn of the 19th century, the clothing industries were some of the key trades to be transformed by the Industrial Revolution. As a result, many of the clothing workers who had plied their trades in or near their homes came to be grouped together into large factories. They led the way—often unwillingly—for the transformation of modern life.

Cloth Finishers

A variety of artisans have worked through the ages to prepare woven cloth for use by the *tailor* or *dressmaker*. Most prominent of these cloth finishers have been *dyers*, *fullers*, and *shearers*.

The craft of dyeing began thousands of years ago, when people discovered that plants and insects could be used to color human skin and the skins of animals. The Swiss Lake Dwellers of about 2000 B.C. used vegetable dyes. The Chinese had dyeing workshops as early as 3000 B.C.

The major dyes of the ancient world came from plants and insects. *Indigo*, which produced blue, was a plant cultivated in India and Egypt as well as by the Incas of Peru. *Woad*, also a blue plant dye, grew in the Near East, England, and Gaul (ancient France). The ancient

Romans wrote of the Celts in England who used woad to paint themselves blue in order to scare their enemies. *Madder* is a red dye plant that was used in the ancient world. Mummies in Egyptian tombs have been found wrapped in linen dyed with madder. Insects were also sources of red dye. *Cochineal*, an insect found in Mexico, and *kermes*, from the Near East, produced crimson dyes. These were precious dyes, as it takes 70,000 dried insects to produce one pound of cochineal. Another red dye came from the *lac* insect, related to cochineal and kermes. This insect, which is also the source of shellac, is found in India, Burma, Indochina, and Thailand. *Lichen* plants found in Sweden, Scotland, Norway, and Ireland color woolens different shades of brown, red, yellow, and purple; some of these lichens are used even today to create the misty colors of Harris tweed.

The most famous dye of the ancient world was *Tyrian purple*, actually a variety of shades from deep red to

In early times dyers often performed other cloth-finishing functions as well, including pressing and smoothing the cloth, readying it for tailors. (By Jost Amman, from The Book of Trades, *late 16th century)*

almost black. This purple dye came from a tiny sea snail found in the Mediterranean Sea off the Phoenician coast. Because each snail gave up only a minute amount of the dye, Tyrian purple was precious, expensive, and thus reserved for church and state rulers. From this dye comes the phrase "born to the purple," meaning of the royal birth. In some periods, it was even a capital offense (one punishable by death) for commoners to wear the *royal purple*.

The art of dyeing developed in secrecy in the ancient world. Recipes for dyes were passed on only to sons or other close relatives. By 715 B.C., however, wool dyeing in Rome was established as a profession. According to the ancient Greek historian Plutarch, in that year the king of Rome, Numa Pompilius, established a *Collegium Tinctorium* to develop the industry and share the secrets. The Romans knew many different dyes and also held the secret of *colorfast dyes*, those that kept their original colors instead of running or fading. The dyes they used were divided into *major dyes* and *minor dyes*. Major dyes were used generally for the clothes of both men and women. Minor dyes were divided into those colors used exclusively for men's clothes and those for women's clothes. When the Roman Empire fell in the fifth century A.D. the art and secrets of dyeing were, for the most part, lost in the chaos and warfare of the Dark Ages.

When the craft revived, later in the Middle Ages, dyers often organized into guilds. In the German states, there were three groups of *dyeing guilds*. The lowest class was the *plain dyers*, who used simple colors and worked from 4 A.M. to 7 P.M. The plain dyers included apprentices who had to spend three years working in a dye shop, then four more as journeymen, traveling around to various cloth shops in Germany in order to produce the "master piece" of dyed wool that was their entrance into the higher levels of their craft. The higher levels included dyers of "high colors" and expert dyers who were so skilled that they were able to work independently of guild rules.

Dyeing during the Middle Ages was not only skilled but also heavy work; it was almost always done by men. The dyer and his assistants circled around large vats, turning over the wool or cloth with long poles as they went by. But not all societies in the Middle Ages recognized dyers as professionals. In France they were contemptuously referred to as "blue nails" because they stained their hands with their work. Dyers were refused admission to the clothing guilds in France. In Florence, Italy, in 1193, the cloth guilds forbade the establishment of a dyers' guild. Many of the dyers left Florence for Genoa and Lucca, where guilds for dyers flourished. In England, dyers were considered *weavers' assistants*. Although a craft guild for weavers was established in England in 1164, it was not until 1188 that the dyers were able to form their own guilds.

Shearers raised the nap on cloth and then smoothed it by cutting it; often they doubled as cleaners. (By Jost Amman, from The Book of Trades, *late 16th century)*

The guild system that controlled the dyeing industry in Europe had rigid rules concerning quality and pay, and was closely watched by government. One necessary role that government regulation played was control of the water supply. Water was a necessary ingredient in every dye recipe. But because most dyeshops were small in scale and operated out of the homes or cottages of the workers, the rules and regulations were often sidestepped. One rule often broken was that requiring the use of woad in preference to indigo to dye cloth blue. Dyers could see that indigo gave a better tint and preferred to use the imported indigo rather than locally-grown woad.

From the Middle Ages to the late 19th century the dyeing industry changed very little. The dyers welcomed the new colors and exotic dyestuffs that explorers brought back with them from the East. They integrated these dyestuffs into their traditional recipes and passed them down to new generations of guild members. During the 18th century many of these recipes became standardized. Even the apparatus used by dyers changed very little until the 20th century, when the industry became mechanized and the wooden vats were replaced by stainless steel.

The biggest change in the dyeing industry happened in 1856 when W.H. Perkin, an English chemist, discovered a way of manufacturing *synthetic dyes*, that is, dyes produced in the laboratory rather than from plants and animals. Perkin's discovery of the first *aniline dye* distilled from coal tar not only changed the dyeing industry but also influenced the fashions of the day. The dye he created was a purplish color known as *mauve* and it became all the rage, especially after Queen Victoria wore a mauve dress at the Great Exhibition of 1862.

By the end of the 19th century most natural dyes had been replaced by the more dependable synthetic dyes. The switch to the synthetics was further solidified during World War I when the German dye industry, which supplied most of the Western world, was shut down. The

These Chinese dyers, like their kin elsewhere, had to work near large and steady supplies of water. (From G. Waldo Browne's The New America and the Far East, *1901)*

dyeing industry, which began in agriculture, continued in the chemist's laboratory.

Further processes in the finishing of cloth were fulling and shearing. *Fullers* cleaned, scoured, stretched, and raised the nap of the newly woven cloth. Fulling was an arduous yet unskilled task that involved trampling the cloth in a trough filled with water, which served to shrink it, and then stretching it smooth and even on hooks to a precise length and breadth. The stretching process, known as *tentering*, has remained in our language; the expression "on tenterhooks" means being kept in a state of suspense or uncertainty. After the cloth was stretched, if the fullers had not already raised the nap, *shearers* would do so and then shear or cut the nap to give the finished cloth a smooth surface.

Frescoes in the ruins of Pompeii depict fullers at work shrinking cloth in troughs by trampling on it with their feet. There were guilds for fullers among the Romans in ancient times as well as throughout Europe during the Middle Ages. Like the dyers, fullers found it helpful to organize in order to secure the water supplies that were so essential to their work. In Flanders fullers and shearers, like dyers, usually worked on their own

These fullers are using teasels to raise the soft, fuzzy nap on the woven fabric. (From Diderot's Encyclopedia, late 18th century)

premises, owning their own equipment and employing others as assistants and apprentices. Fulling and tentering was paid for by the piece. Shearing and dyeing prices depended upon the dyes that were used in the cloth. Shearers used shears that were three or four feet long. These shears were so valuable that they were often mentioned in the wills of shearers.

In the great cloth finishing industry in Italy, fullers, like dyers, were often subservient to the main guilds and not allowed to form their own. Rich and powerful clothiers would buy unfinished cloths at the great cloth fairs of Europe, such as those of Champagne, and then put them out to dyers and fullers to finish, paying the workers by the piece.

During the 11th and 12th centuries in England fulling mills were introduced, in which waterpower replaced manpower. The job that the fuller had once done with his feet was now done by two wooden hammers which were alternately raised and dropped upon the cloth, using the *tilt hammer system*, which employed a revolving drum attached to the spindle of a water wheel. The fullers complained bitterly about this innovation, pointing out that it resulted in inferior work as well as unemployment.

But their protests were futile and by the 14th century fulling mills were widespread in the textile industry.

In England the mills helped bring about the movement of the textile industry from the urban centers to the countryside, especially to the West Country, in order to take advantage of the waterpower of the rivers. This helped free the industry from the restrictions of the urban guilds and the high taxes of the towns. Access to waterpower, freedom from restrictions, and lower costs opened up the industry to the mechanical innovations that would later become known as the Industrial Revolution.

For related occupations in this volume, *Clothiers*, see the following:
 Fiber Workers
 Spinners
 Tailors and Dressmakers
 Weavers

For related occupations in other volumes of the series, see the following:
in *Harvesters*:
 Farmers
 Fishers

Fiber Workers

Before fibers can be spun into yarn they must be cleaned and separated. Each of the four major natural fibers—flax, cotton, wool, and silk—has its own preparation process and its own specialists, including *combers*, *carders*, and other fiber workers.

Flax was most likely the first plant used for fiber. As early as 8000 B.C. flax was grown by the Swiss Lake Dwellers. These people must have discovered that once the fiber is separated from the plant it can be woven. Woven flax is called *linen*, a strong material that holds up well in water and has a characteristic called *wicking* that moves moisture to its surface. Because of its wicking ability, linen is a clean and comfortable material to wear.

After the flax plant has grown for 100 days, it is pulled up, roots and all, and tied into bundles that are left to dry in the fields. Once dried, the flax has its seeds removed by *rippling*, that is, drawing the heads of the plant through a comb, or by *threshing* (beating) the dried stalks with a heavy tool to remove the seeds. The seedless stalks are then tied into bundles and stored.

The next step in the flax-working process is *retting*, or decomposing the pectins and gums that hold the plant fibers together. There are several ways of doing this. Some early societies spread the stalks out on dewy fields and left them for several weeks. Some immersed the bundles in ponds or slow-running rivers. In our own time flax is retted in tanks of water that are carefully prepared and controlled. These modern tanks are not all that different, though, from those in ancient Egypt, in which the flax was kept immersed in water provided by long lines of slaves who formed a bucket brigade to bring water from the river Nile.

After the plant gums have rotted away, the flax can be broken. Breaking is a pounding operation that frees the fibers from the woody stems. The flax is laid across a tool known as a *brake*, and the brake's upper blade is brought down sharply. Then the stalks are tapped with a wooden knife, in a process called *scutching* or *swingling*, to remove particles of the stem. Next the stalks are *hackled* (also known as *hatchelled* or *heckled*)—that is, combed by being pulled through a series of boards with protruding pairs of pins of different sizes. The fibers are divided into long ones, known as *line* (as in linen), and short ones called *tow*. The fiber is then ready to be spun.

Ancient Egypt was known as the land of linen. Linen production was a major industry, with state-operated centers using slave labor. Many slaves (often prisoners of war) suffered working conditions comparable to modern sweatshops. Linen symbolized divine light and purity to the Egyptians, and it was the only fiber worn by priests. Flax retted in the waters of the Nile was said to be softer than flax retted anywhere else in the world.

The Hebrews are said to have learned the process of preparing flax for spinning and weaving during their captivity in Egypt. They wore linen undergarments beneath their woolen robes. The Jews believed that those who wore linen next to their skin were less likely to contract leprosy than those who wore wool. Charlemagne, too, understood the sanitary nature of linen due to its wicking property. During the eighth century A.D. he ordered each family in his realm to learn to process, spin, and weave flax because of its purity. He also saw a possible market in the production of linen for Christian liturgical vestments.

During the Middle Ages, Flanders became the center of the European linen industry. Labor was skilled and the climate was ideal for growing flax. Linen manufacture in Ireland dates from the Normans, who settled there in the seventh century A.D. It has continued into the 20th century, especially among the Protestants of Northern Ireland. The factory system of linen production took over the linen industry in Belfast early in the 19th century. This destroyed the small-scale linen producers who had made the fabric in their homes in what was called a cottage industry.

Cotton, too, is a plant fiber. The process of preparing cotton for spinning is much simpler than that for flax. It is merely necessary to remove the dirt, leaves, and other useless material from the boll and then to separate the fibers called *lint*, from the seeds. For 5,000 years this was done by hand. In India during the Middle Ages, a *roller gin* was invented to clean the seeds from the cotton. By rotating two closely set rollers, one could draw the cotton lint through but force out the seed. This was a slow process, but it was used successfully until 1793, when Eli Whitney, an American inventor, designed the *cotton saw gin*.

Once the cotton fibers have been cleaned, they must be *carded*, that is, straightened and disentangled. This can be done by hand-pulling the fibers into little bunches. In India, bows were used to fluff the fibers and remove the dirt and knots. The worker struck the taut string of the bow with a mallet. The vibrations of the bow then fluffed

In Asia, bows like these were used from ancient times to fluff, clean, and straighten cotton fibers. (From Picturesque Palestine)

the cotton. The use of *combs* to align the fibers was not widely practiced until the 19th century.

India was considered the cradle of cotton from earliest times. Processing cotton was an individual activity, done in the home. The processing methods were already developed by 1500 B.C., and little change was made in the industry until 20th-century attempts to industrialize it. Cotton was not a major fiber in the European medieval textile industry because of spinning and supply

As in ancient times, early American workers threshed cotton using a simple bow. (From Diderot's Encyclopedia, *late 18th century)*

problems. Cotton from the American continents solved these problems. American cotton was longer and stronger than Indian cotton. When machines revolutionized the textile industry in the 18th and 19th centuries, cotton grew in popularity, partly because of its strength. Cotton produced in industrial factories was also cheaper, because cotton workers were not, at first, well organized in unions. As a result they were paid less than the better-organized wool workers.

Wool is an animal fiber, shorn or clipped from living sheep. It must first be washed and scoured of grease, dried perspiration, and excrement. Then the wool is picked to clean burrs and plant leaves out of it. Picking is now a mechanical process, but in ancient times the wool was spread out on mesh and beaten with sticks.

The wool fibers, like cotton fibers, must be aligned before the wool can be spun into yarn. This process, no matter how it is done, is known as *carding*. Wool can be carded using the fingers, a bow (in the same way that cotton was first ginned in India), or the prickly part of teasel or thistle plants. The term *carding* comes from the Latin word *carduus*, which means thistle. In France during the 13th century, hand cards were first made with teeth of bent metal wire to card the wool. Today wool is carded by machine.

For most woolens, carding is the last stage before the wool is spun into yarn. But for *worsted*, a long fine wool yarn, there is another step known as *combing* which smooths the fibers. In ancient Rome, combs were first

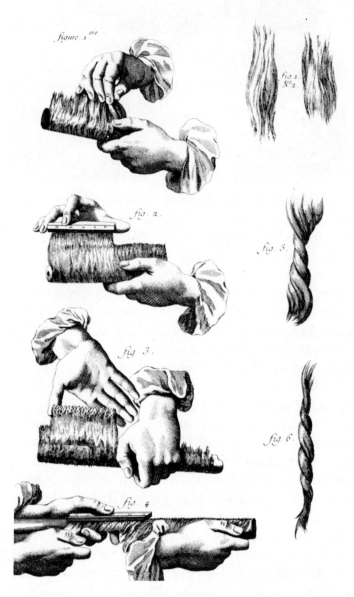

The process of combing and carding cotton remained the same for many centuries. (From Diderot's Encyclopedia, *late 18th century)*

made of iron teeth set into a wooden frame. Until the 19th century, combing was a skilled hand operation. The combs were heated and used two at a time to create the small, smooth, lustrous yarn that is named *worsted* after the English town of Worstead where much of it was made.

In shops like these—though normally less airy—combers and carders worked to grade and prepare wool for use. (From Diderot's Encyclopedia, *late 18th century)*

Wool was first developed as a textile fiber in Mesopotamia, the land between the Tigris and Euphrates rivers. It became a favorite fabric throughout the ancient world, worn by most people who lived in the ancient civilizations of Greece and Rome. By the first century A.D. there was already a wool-combers' guild at Brixia and a wool-carders' guild at Brixellum in northern Italy. When Rome fell during the fifth century A.D., the wool industry reverted to a cottage industry. Wool production continued in the cottages through the early Middle Ages. In Flanders the carders, combers, and spinners were independent and unorganized, working out of their homes. At the same time in Italy, combers and carders suffered more restriction. They worked in textile shops under strict supervision, were paid by the hour, and often had an uncertain future. Laws forbade them to organize to improve their lot.

In France during the 12th and 13th centuries, cloth making was set up in what would later be called a capitalist system. The factory would be owned by a wealthy person such as a *draper*, who hired others to do the actual labor. In the sorting house the humblest workers would sort, wash, and beat wool in large tubs of water. When it had dried, the wool would be carded or combed, and then sent out to the workers in their homes to be spun into thread.

In England the wool industry developed extensively during the late Middle Ages. A sack of wool weighing 240 pounds would employ more than 60 persons for a week to manufacture it into cloth: three men to sort, dry, and mix it, making it ready for the carders; five to scribble it (card it coarsely); 35 women and girls to card and spin it; eight men to weave it; four to spool it; and eight to scour, mill, pack, and press it.

If the wool was to be made into the fine yarn known as worsted, it would be sent to the shop of the *wool comber*. Wool combing was said to have been invented by the Bishop Blaize, a saint of the fourth or fifth century, who is honored as the patron saint of the trade. Wool combers celebrated his feast on the third of February. Wool used for making worsted was first washed by the wool comber and then dried by twisting it around a fixed hook. An important tool of the wool comber's trade was the *comb pot*, a jar of clay under which a fire of the best charcoal burned. The combs, made of a highly tempered steel (steel that had been hardened by heating and cooling it), were heated in the comb pot. When the combs were hot, the wool comber combed the dried wool until it was fine and smooth. Usually four wool combers would work at the same pot. They would be paid by the piece and, in the early 19th century, could earn from 16 to 20 shillings per week.

The English wool combers had a reputation for enjoying time off from their jobs. They might come in on Monday morning, light the fire underneath the comb pot and then go away until Wednesday or even Thursday. The wool combers had a strong sense of fellowship. When one was out of work, he would set out in search of a new master; this was called "going on the tramp." At every shop where he would call, he would be given one penny if there was no job. The pennies were raised by the wool combers who worked in the shop. Each shop also provided a spare bench, where people on the tramp could rest themselves.

In 1738 the first *wool carding mill* was set up in England, in Birmingham. It lasted just two-and-a-half years, meeting little success and much opposition. Two versions of a *carding machine* were patented in 1748, but disaster, in the form of fire, hit them both. Later in the century, as the spinning machines of Hargreaves and Arkwright caught on, the carding machine became inevitable, and the old ones were improved. Although at first the manufacturers of woolens would take the wool to be carded and then pass it out to be spun by others, soon the mills grew and consolidated all the processes in wool production under the one roof of the factory.

Silk is a fiber that is manufactured by silkworms, caterpillar-like insects that feed on mulberry leaves and spin cocoons that can be unraveled into thread. The Chinese first perfected the process of softening the *sericin*, the gummy protein that holds the silk cocoon together, by boiling the cocoons in water and then loosening the filaments and pulling them from the cocoons. This process, known as *reeling*, is still done by hand because it requires skill and delicacy to unroll the filaments, which can be up to 1,000 yards in length. Each filament is thinner at its beginning and end, and the filaments must be joined carefully to form a continuous thread. Twisting the filaments together into silk thread is known as *throwing* silk. *Spun silk* is made by carding, combing, and spinning waste silk into a thread or yarn.

The Chinese kept the secret of the silkworm to themselves for centuries. During the Han dynasty (202 B.C.-220 A.D.), the Chinese raised silkworms and reeled silk as they had done for centuries and would continue to do for future centuries. Silk making was a woman's industry, carried on in the home. In silk-producing provinces of China, the daughters, mothers, and grandmothers of every family spent much of their day for at least six months of the year feeding, tending, and su-

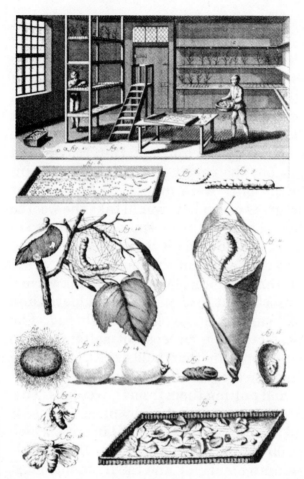

Long held secret in China, techniques of sericulture came to be practiced around the world. (From Diderot's Encyclopedia, *late 18th century)*

pervising the silkworms as well as unraveling, spinning, weaving, dyeing, and embroidering the silk.

Silkworms are temperamental creatures who demand close attention. The temperature of the environment in which they live must be constant. The mulberry leaves they eat must be fresh and chopped. They must eat every half hour. They are repelled by drafts, loud noises—even thunder—and strong smells, such as fish, meat, and sweat. When the silkworms were ready to start spinning their cocoons, the women of the house placed them on trays of rice straw and kept them in a mild heat. The women would watch the silkworms spinning their cocoons closely and, just a moment before a cocoon was

complete, they would throw it into boiling water to dissolve the gum and kill the silkworm. After that they beat the water with branches, catching the cocoons in the twigs. Then, carefully and gently, the women unraveled the cocoons and twisted the fine threads together to make a single strand.

For many centuries taxes in China had to be paid in lengths of silk, so that a household's future was in its women's hands. They had to be patient, diligent, and economical, often working by moonlight in order to save fuel. Silk was the symbol of womanhood—even the empress herself attended to a silkworm-rearing house.

The silk industry was introduced into the West during the sixth-century reign of the Emperor Justinian, reportedly by monks who smuggled in the silkworm eggs hidden in bamboo canes. The Moslems brought silkworms to Spain and Sicily in the ninth and tenth centuries. By the 13th century, Italy—with its mild climate and skilled textile workers, as well as its wealthy traders and bankers—had become the silk center of the Western world.

All Chinese women, including empresses, traditionally occupied themselves in feeding silkworms and sorting their cocoons. (From G. Waldo Browne's The New America and the Far East, *1901)*

Although silk-weaving did not begin in France until the 15th century, the French silk industry soon rivaled the Italian. It was a cottage industry, not unlike that in China. The work was shared by men, women, and children. The women unwound the cocoons, spun the thread and rolled it onto spools; the men did the weaving; the children helped their parents in all of the tasks. Peasant women would then carry cocoons around in their bodices to keep them safe and warm. The silk-making craft was handed down like a legacy from generation to generation. It increased and prospered in France, especially in Lyon.

Silk manufacturing was closely tied to fashion. During the Renaissance period in France, when styles were flamboyant and quick to change, there was never enough silk. But by 1789, when fashion turned to the printed cotton fabrics imported from Persia or India, there were 20,000 unemployed silk workers on public welfare in Lyon.

In the late 19th century the Lyon Chamber of Commerce sent a trade mission to China to investigate its silk industry. They found almost every family in the province of Szechuan, from the richest to the poorest,

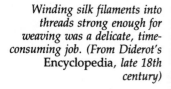

Winding silk filaments into threads strong enough for weaving was a delicate, time-consuming job. (From Diderot's Encyclopedia, *late 18th century)*

engaged in the raising of silkworms. Still operated as a cottage industry, the volume of silk production was low—only one or two ounces per family at most. Innovation in the industry was not encouraged. The methods of the Chinese did not impress the more sophisticated silk authorities from France. They had come not so much in the interests of industrial espionage as to introduce their own ways to China. But the Chinese silk industry soon fell victim to silkworm disease and the lack of technological innovation.

As China grew weaker, Japan grew stronger as a silk-producing nation. In the early 20th century, the West imported about one-quarter of its silk from China and a similar amount from Japan. By 1930 Japan had become the leader in world silk production, with 40 percent of Japanese peasant families raising silkworms. *Filatures*—silk factories—bought the cocoons from the peasants and employed their daughters in the factories, where the most up-to-date methods were used. From Japan, industrialization and the new technology spread to China, especially in and around Canton and Shanghai.

But the breakdown of the cottage industry and the rise of the factory system brought the abuses that are associated with industrialization. Child labor was rife; in Shanghai a third of the labor force was made up of children, many younger than six. The air in a *filature* was hot and humid. Fainting and, after a long period of exposure, tuberculosis, were widespread among adults as well as children.

War, civil as well as global, changed the silk-manufacturing industry in China and Japan. Yet an even more devastating fate befell them in the mid-20th century—the introduction of nylon and other synthetic fibers. The synthetics were inexpensive as well as quick-drying and long-lasting. Many of them required little or no ironing. But silk workers—most of them still in Asian countries—continued to supply the precious threads for affluent buyers around the world, as silk-working became a luxury industry.

For related occupations in this volume, *Clothiers*, see the following:
    Cloth Finishers
    Spinners
    Weavers

For related occupations in other volumes of the series, see the following:
in *Harvesters:*
    Farmers
in *Scholars and Priests:*
    Priests

Hatters

Hatters are the artisans who make men's hats. Their trade developed separately from that of the *milliners*, who make women's hats.

The earliest headgear in the ancient world was the *headband*, plain or elegant, worn by men and women to hold back their hair. Aristocrats in Egypt protected their heads with rigid black wigs; an encircling band of gold kept the wig in place. The peoples of Mesopotamia (roughly modern-day Iraq) introduced *turbans* and cone-shaped *miters* for the nobility; the low-born just covered their heads with caps. The *kyrbasia* (now called a *bashlik*) of Persia (now Iran) was the first hat to be made from felt and with a crown, a rounded summit; it often included ear flaps that could be tied under the chin.

The ancient Greeks generally wore hats only for protection against the weather, when traveling or working outdoors. Travelers wore the *petasus*, a low, round, and broad hat that had not only a crown, but also the first brim. Hermes, messenger of the gods, was often portrayed wearing a petasus with a small pair of wings that grew from the crown. The petasus and crude leather caps were the main head coverings in Europe through the days of the Roman Empire and for the first seven centuries of the Middle Ages.

In the 15th century men began wearing the *coif*, a cloth cap that was pulled down snug over the skull. On top of this, a man could wear a hat, just as shoes are worn over socks. Body heat was precious in those days, when the indoors stayed almost as cold as the outdoors. People wanted to wear layers of insulation, and taking off a hat counted as a small sacrifice. Men would do so only as a token of honor to the great; this token survived in the courtly habit of tipping one's hat to show respect. As Europe's prosperity increased, those with the money were able to select from a new array of hats. These could denote rank, usually by the lavishness of their decoration. Some hats even indicated a person's profession; the flat *mortarboard,* for example, came to be worn by college teachers during these years.

Throughout this period, we know virtually nothing about the people who made the hats or prepared the felt used in hats and other items, such as slippers, gloves, or caps. Certainly caps of felt date back into the Bronze Age in Eurasia. In Roman times some workshops apparently specialized in making felt hats and other goods. But the sparse records we have about hatters themselves date back only a few centuries. A 15th-century source mentions the availability of "fyne felt hats or spectacles to neede." An English village lists among its inhabitants in 1465 "Majoria Claton, Cappeknytter." A royal proclamation of 1488 mentions hatters as a profession, with a hint at their prosperity: "Hatmakers and Kapmakers doth sell their hattes and cappes at such an outrageous price." The *Anatomie of Abuses,* published in 1586, condemned hat vanity. Fashionable people felt compelled to order hats with "a greate bunche of feathers of divers and sundrie colors, peakying on top of their heads, not unlike cockescombes."

By far most of the hats for men were made from felt. A substance derived from fur, felt could be molded, but also cut and sewn like cloth. Most hatters made their own felt, and by the 17th century the hatter and the *felt maker* seem to have been looked on as one and the same.

Beaver skin was the hatter's favorite fur. Dried, it was called *plew*, from which came the name *pelt*, meaning the skin of a fur-bearing animal. The hatter wet the fur to make it easier to comb, or *card*. After this, the pelts were piled on a bench to dry. Next, the *bower* went to work. He took the pelts to a small alcove, with one high-placed window for light to work by. Dangling from the ceiling

Felt was a favored material of hatters, not only for hats but also for caps and even slippers. (By Jost Amman, from The Book of Trades, *late 16th century)*

was his *bow*, shaped much like that for a musical instrument, but far longer and stouter. The bower held the bow's catgut strings against the fur, vibrating the catgut with his *bow-pin*. The fur flew loose, settling into a level, oval pile—a *batt*—approximately the amount used to make one hat. The now-loose fibers then had to be molded together. The batt was covered with damp linen, which was weighted down by a *basket*, which looked like a washboard with a handle at its center. First, the fur became matted; with enough pressure, it could be fused together into felt.

The fashioning of the hat then started. First, a batt of felt was wrapped around a paper triangle and sealed in place by a second damp cloth, wrapped around it, which the hatter pressed in tight with his fingers. The result was a solid frame; the hat was built from this *body*.

The hat's body was larger than any human head. The fur's fibers, though turned into felt, had to be still further compacted. To accomplish this, the hat's body was boiled in a vat of water for about seven hours. After this, the hatter shaped the body by hand, working it on shelves atop a boiling kettle, for steam kept the felt pliable. The hatter smoothed the distribution of fur, even using a brush to paste on handfuls where a bare spot called for them. Once allowed to cool off, the body shrank by half, its felt becoming thicker as it contracted. Next followed the procedure called rolling it off; this actually meant rolling the fur in more tightly. The body could be rolled on horsehair; fiber that still stuck up afterwards was sliced off.

The hatter then folded and fitted the body over a wood block for molding, with string tied about its top; the hatter pushed the string down, pressing the body closer against the block. A small, blunt tool made of wood or bone was used to smooth and polish the felt. Felt that hung below the block was folded up into a brim. Slicing off the string, the hatter placed the body on a flat board; the brim was then smoothed out with a special tool called a *brim tolliker*.

The hat had been shaped from felt and given its final form. Only finishing work remained. The fur was combed again and dried in an oven; then it was dyed and coated with shellac, or sometimes glue (also made in the workshop), for durability. The hatter backtracked briefly in his work; the hat had to be softened in a metal box filled with steam, then put back on the block to firm up its shape. After that came ironing and rubbing with a piece of pumice for smoothness, a process called *pouncing*. A circle of leather was sewn around the inner crown, just above the brim, and the hat was complete. Any further work was just "dressing," or decoration.

Samuel Pepys, a 17th-century English government official whose diary has become a famous source of information about day-to-day life at that time, noted that in London a beaver hat cost from four to six pounds, or 50 to 70 dollars today. The price is not surprising, given the

Hatters—in French, chapeliers—went through all of the stages of beating and fulling the material used in hatmaking. (From Diderot's Encyclopedia, *late 18th century*)

long and complex manufacturing process. Felt making itself was thought to be demeaning, since it meant tedious physical labor and exposure to steam. But, a writer of the day remarked, it was rewarded with "great pay." Europe's affluent needed felt for their hats and did not worry much about cost. Hatmaking in late 17th-century England benefited much from the influx of Huguenot refugees from the European continent who, said one reporter, were "skilled in preparing the beaver and sticking it to the hat."

In this period, hatters and feltmakers formed organizations much like the guilds that had their roots in earlier times. They had a patron saint, St. Clement, who traditionally was supposed to have discovered feltmaking after he lined his sandals with rabbit's fur and found them, at the end of a long trek, matted together into a firm mass. In truth, modern guild practices often had more to do with social than industrial relations, as witness the initiation a young hatmaker at the turn of the 19th century:

When a young man came up to London and got employment for the first time, the first claim made upon him by his shopmates...was 10s. [shillings] for a "maiden garnish." All the men who partook of this [drinking spree] paid...a contribution...If the number was small, the inebriety would be large...From these and a variety of other circumstances...it was not surprising that the old felt-hatters were proverbial in their intemperate habits.

When Europeans came to the Americas, they brought with them their hatmaking skills. Indeed, hatmaking would have an enormous influence on the opening of North America—both Canada and the western United States—since many of the earliest explorers were fur trappers following the steadily retreating beaver population. When the *Mayflower* sailed back from America to London in 1621, it carried two barrels of beaver skins.

The Pilgrims exported 20 barrels in 1634. European settlers traded with the Native Americans and then made profits from the merchants back home. The more ragged and worn a skin was, the more easily its fur could be turned into felt. The Native Americans *tanned* pelts, first by soaking them in bear grease and then pounding them with rocks. This produced first-rate hatter's material. In 1657, the Dutch colonies in America sold 40,000 skins to Europe. By 1664 England had seized the territory and the trade.

The Virginia Assembly voted in 1662 to reward each hat made in the colony with 10 pounds of tobacco, the colony's chief crop. By the 18th-century, much of the Colonies' fur flowed to native hatters. These artisans passed Virginia by, gathering most densely where the furs were sold: Pennsylvania, New Jersey, New York, and the colonies of New England. The Northeast was also nearer to the northern forests—and so to the beavers' main range. Ten hatters lived in early 18th-century Boston; each made an average of 40 hats a week. In 1788, 124 hatters marched in Philadelphia's July 4th procession; they made, in 1790, over 31,600 felt hats and 7,600 wool hats. Pennsylvania hatters altogether made over 54,200 felt hats and 161,100 of wool that same year—and Pennsylvania was only one of the American states making hats. The market for the more expensive grades shrank outside the city, but most hats were made and sold domestically (within the Colonies rather than in Europe). In 1790 American exported only 668 hats, at a collective value of $1,392.

The Americans made beaver hats of three grades, varying according to the quality of fur used. The cheapest model, a fur-napped felt hat, used rabbit's fur as its foundation but came covered with either wool or beaver fur. It cost seven dollars and was advertised as "never wearing out." Beavers had been hunted almost to extinction by the 1820s. To conserve their supply, hatters patched felt with fur from sheep, otters, goats, rabbits, seals, and even muskrats.

In the Industrial Age, hatters and felt-makers began to move from being relatively independent artisans in small workshops, where each had a chance to learn all the skills and to advance in the trade, to *factory workers* confined to narrow specialties for much of their lives. A small New England town, Danbury, Connecticut, saw the first hatters' factory in 1780. The factory was worked, at the beginning, by only one hatter with a journeyman and two apprentices. But it soon grew. Danbury became an industrial center, turning out more hats than anywhere else in the United States, probably in the world. A French traveler visited the American factories early in the 19th century and reported that they worked faster and more efficiently than any workshop in Europe. In 1836, the combined sales by 245 hatters in Newark, New Jersey, came to more than a million dollars.

William Rankin and Associates was one of the largest hatters' firms in the United States, employing 600 to 700 workers. Steam engines heated their irons, pulverized wood, and manufactured dye from the chips. Furs could be stripped by machine, requiring only four men to do a job that formerly took 30. The factory stocked up on furs, keeping a reserve worth up to $30,000.

Prices came down as production rose. John Nicholas Genin, a hatter who won awards for his work, listed his prices in an 1850 catalogue. His finest beaver hat cost $4.50, $2.50 less than a fur-napped hat of 60 years before. He sold a second-grade beaver hat for $3.50, moleskin caps of two grades, and finally three grades of cheaper cloth caps, at $2.00, $1.50, and $1.00. In 1846 H.A. Wells patented a "felting machine," which took over the work of the bowers, sorting loose fur fibers and producing 400 hat bodies in one day. The labor cost of making a hat body dropped by more than 75 percent.

Finishers in hat factories were exposed to at least one severe industrial hazard. The fur was processed with nitrate of mercury. The finisher's work, rubbing hot irons across felt, released the mercury as vapor that the finisher breathed in. The result was nerve damage often

Finishers were sometimes made "mad as a hatter" by exposure to mercury, which caused neurological problems. (From Phillips' Book of English Trades, 1823)

characterized by the "hatter's shakes," which probably gave rise to the popular phrase "mad as a hatter." Ventilation largely cured this problem later.

Not all hats were made of felt, however. In modern times, Asia and Latin America entered the international hatmaking trade with hats of various fibers. The Philippine Islands, in the early 20th century, made an average of two million hats a year, many for export. These hatters had their work sold, according to one source, in "the United States, the United Kingdom, Japan, France, Italy, Spain, China...and before the recent World War to Germany and Austria-Hungary." The Philippine hatmakers worked as artisans; they stayed hatters rather than become factory hands. Thousands of people were able to earn their livings at this trade.

Many of these hats were woven, and it helped that dozens of different fiber-bearing plants grew in the Philippines. The islands' climate also helped, since rain and wet keep fibers supple, allowing them to be more easily woven. During a dry spell, Philippine *hat weavers* would sometimes climb down into abandoned wells to continue their work. The hatters demanded their pay before working; this, the source noted, "often results in the workers becoming more or less bound to the brokers [merchants] who commissioned and sold the hats from debt, for debt by the native code of honor is a thing that must be paid."

To make their hats, the Filipinos first stripped leaves from palm trees. Usable fibers could be drawn from the stems of the leaves and from the leaves themselves. These fibers had to be flattened out, rolled with the palm of the hand, and then boiled in vinegar and water for up to five days. They came out firm but pliable, ready for weaving. The Filipinos shaped hats for their own use, with low crowns and broad brims, by weaving alone. When merchants found buyers abroad, the hatters started fitting their work on blocks. Finishers trimmmed the edges. Then, after the hats had been cleaned and dried, they could be delivered to the merchants.

The Filipino hat weavers and their counterparts in Latin America were the last hatters to compete with the hat factory. Their work sold abroad as sometimes useful novelties. A *balibuntal* from the Philippines or a *panama* hat from Latin America might keep off the sun during vacation, but few Europeans would wear one as part of their daily attire. Factory-made hats of felt or wool are still the most frequently worn. Steadily improving machines took over every step of the hatter's work—so much so that even 50 years ago a hat manufacturer might boast that it *still* employed some workers who relied on their own skill and judgment: "That is where...superior...quality is really *made*." To hand-roll

While making felt toppers for fine gentlemen, hatters themselves often wore paper hats, at least in 19th-century England. (Authors' archives)

felt hat bodies—just one stage of the hatter's old craft—workers now needed "skill and experience of the highest order of the hatter's art."

Hatters and felt makers were among the earliest factory workers to attempt to organize labor unions. In the United States, hat finishers' organizing efforts date back to at least the 1850s. Not until the 20th century, however, were successful unions—such as the United Cloth Hat and Cap Makers' International Union —established. Even so, the number of skilled workers was falling, as machines took over more of the trade and as felt became more widely used for commercial and industrial purposes, such as insulation and carpeting.

Eventually the much-reduced numbers of hatters joined forces in the United States with the milliners, the makers of women's hats, to form the United Hatters, Cap and Millinery Workers' International Union. (Most of the hatters were men and most of the milliners were women.) Both types of workers have been much affected by modern casual fashions in which hats are less important than they once were. Such classic felt hats as the famous derby and homburg, and even the fez or beret, are not very common today. Hatters can only hope that the pendulum of style will in the future swing their way once again.

For related occupations in this volume, *Clothiers*, see the following:

Cloth Finishers
Fiber Workers
Milliners
Shoemakers and Other Leatherworkers
Tailors and Dressmakers

For related occupations in other volumes of the series, see the following:
in *Financiers and Traders*:
   Merchants and Shopkeepers
in *Harvesters*:
   Hunters
in *Manufacturers and Miners*:
   Factory Workers

Milliners

The making of hats for women grew up as a craft independently of men's hatmaking. In medieval times, women's hats were assembled and sold by *haberdashers*, those merchants who specialized in accessories of dress such as feathers, buttons, and laces. In the Middle Ages the source of these articles of adornment was often Milan, in northern Italy, then the center of fashion and the fashion trade. Because their wares so often came from Milan, haberdashers became known as *Milaners*, a term which soon became *milliners*.

Haberdashers were an important group of merchants, especially in the 12th and 13th centuries. Their guild was one of the "Great Twelve" in London and, with the other merchant guilds, wielded great social and political power, as well as exercising a virtual monopoly on price and availability of those items it bought and sold. In *The Canterbury Tales*, the famous poem written in the 14th century, Chaucer includes a haberdasher among his pilgrims to Canterbury. With his guild companions—a dyer, a carpenter, a weaver, and a carpetmaker—the haberdasher in the poem is described as displaying his recently acquired wealth in his new clothes, silver-wrought knives, and richly dressed wife.

This pilgrim haberdasher's wealth might have come, in part, from an imported article that was causing a great sensation in these times—the pin. The thorns, skewers, and bone splinters that women had previously used to attach and hold pieces of cloth were primitive compared to the metal pin. (These were straight pins. Though pins with clasps to hold the point in place had been used on occasion since Greco-Roman times, the safety pin was a modern invention.) Because of the large demand and small supply, pins were so expensive that, when they were first introduced, only the rich could afford them. Noblemen had to increase their wives' dress allowances to cover this precious commodity. From this increase comes the term "pin money," extra money that husbands gave to wives for their private purchases.

Women's hats, like most articles of clothing at this time, were generally made at home, either by women in the family or by female servants or slaves. But here and there would emerge women who had a special flair for creating concoctions out of silk and lace and feathers that others were willing to spend their "pin money" on. Using pins and other imported articles to put together ladies' hats, these milliners would travel to the medieval fairs, such as that at Stourbridge near Cambridge in England, to sell their work and size up their competition. These fairs attracted craftspeople and tradespeople from not only the British Isles but also all of Europe and parts of the Middle East.

One of the tradespeople who supplied haberdashers was the *feather worker*, or *plumassier* as she was known in France. Feathers became an important accessory to hats and dresses beginning in the late 16th century, especially at the French court, where fine distinctions in a woman's status in society could be made by the length or curl of a plume on her hat. France, especially Paris, became the center of the fashion world. Although women at this time generally wore hats only for riding or traveling, such hats for noblewomen and other wealthy women had to be at fashion's peak—small, worn over one ear, and adorned either with large feathers or delicate curled ones. The plumassier, who was most often a woman, might own or rent a small shop, its ceiling hung with peacock tails and ostrich plumes. In the back of the shop would be a workroom, where skilled workers would thin and frizz ostrich plumes and clean, cut, and dye the feathers of birds from all over the world.

By the end of the 18th century, hats for women became so essential that the millinery industry grew enormously. No respectable woman would appear outside her home without a hat. (This practice continued throughout the 19th century and well into the 20th.) Straw hats, woven

The plumassier *(featherworker) was a true specialist, thinning, cutting, frizzing, and dyeing plumes for hats and other adornments. (From Diderot's* Encyclopedia, *late 18th century)*

of Leghorn straw imported from Italy, became most fashionable in England and France at this time. Straw plaiting was a feminine industry, done in the home by poor young women, especially in England. By the 1860s, China—with its cheap labor—began to copy Western straw plaiting, thus gaining an entrance into the millinery market.

In Colonial America, most women made their own clothes and hats, producing many of the materials themselves. Small items they needed, such as pins and needles, they purchased from small general stores and wandering peddlers. In Boston and New York, however, there were enough women of wealth and continental tastes to build up a fashion trade. Fashions changed at least every season; styles in hats were said to have changed 17 times between 1784 and 1786.

New fashions were brought to the Colonies from England and Europe in the form of "babies"—small dolls dressed in miniatures of the latest fashions in dresses, coats, and hats. These fashions were then duplicated by dressmakers and milliners. Women who could not afford to buy the latest fashions sewed their own copies of them at home. Later, fashion trends were shown in pictures, in magazines such as *Godey's Ladies' Book*. Many women wore the same hat year after year with slight, or major, changes in color and trimmings to fit the latest fashion as shown in *Godey's*.

An example of the importance of a hat cut to fit the fashion is shown in *Gone With the Wind*, Margaret Mitchell's monumental melodrama of the Civil War South. Scarlett's attempt to trick the imprisoned Rhett Butler into giving her the money to pay Tara's taxes began with her costume. She used her mother's green velvet drapes to sew a dress and topped off her outfit with a fetching bonnet that Melanie had fabricated using the green velvet curtain scraps to re-cover the frame of a battered bonnet. The crowning—or should it be crowing?—touch to this masterpiece was their old rooster's "gorgeous bronze and green-black tail feathers." Initial steps to Scarlett's downfall, it is to be remembered, were the gifts of luxuries such as pins, needles, and buttons, which Rhett Butler brought her through the blockade of the Southern ports. Rhett's gift of a gorgeous green bonnet with "the perkiest of green ostrich plumes" emerged from a hatbox marked "Rue de la Paix." Scarlett's reputation as a fallen woman was sealed when she refused to dye it to match the black mourning clothes she was required to wear as a widow.

As the millinery industry prospered in the United States, two branches of the industry emerged: *retail* and *wholesale*. The retail branch of the millinery industry was made up of small shops, often owned and run by the milliners themselves. These milliners usually dealt directly with their customers, producing hats made-to-order for each customer and designed with the latest fashions in mind. In the United States the earliest milliners were mostly American, English, and French.

Early milliners specialized in hats, but some handled adornments of all kinds. (From Phillips' Book of English Trades, *1823)*

The second branch of the industry, which had a later start but eventually took over the making of hats, was wholesale millinery. Wholesale milliners made thousands of hats, which were then sold to retail *shopowners* and department stores, or to *distributors* (sometimes called *jobbers*) who acted as middlemen supplying these stores. The wholesale millinery business was one of the last to move from home into factory. In Massachusetts, the center of the millinery industry until just after the Civil War, women in the small towns surrounding the industrial centers worked on hats in their homes and were paid by the piece.

In the late 19th century and into the 20th, the city of New York became the center of the millinery industry in the United States, employing 10 percent of the 134,000 milliners scattered across the country (according to the 1910 census). There were 5,800 milliners in Chicago and 3,800 in Philadelphia. Across the Atlantic, London employed 13,700 milliners; Paris, 19,400; Berlin, 4,400. It was said that a good milliner could find work anywhere on the globe.

Whether retail or wholesale, millinery was considered a skilled trade. Even after the invention of the sewing machine in 1846, most of the milliner's work was done by hand. The demands of the craft varied greatly in the different branches of the trade. Retail milliners were prized for their accuracy, delicacy, and taste, while for wholesale workers speed was all important.

Milliners, whether retail or wholesale, were considered the aristocrats of the needle trades, although their high prestige often disguised low pay. Young women were attracted to millinery because it was considered a refined occupation. Many loved the work itself; some cherished the hope of having their own shops someday. The majority of women employed as milliners at the turn of the century were single and under 21; men made up only 10 percent of milliners.

Women at this time wore different kinds of hats for the two seasons in women's hatmaking, winter and summer.

The buying—and thus the making—of hats was concentrated in three months in the spring and three months in the fall. Between these busy seasons most milliners faced unemployment. The seasonal aspect of the industry wreaked havoc on the lives of people employed to make hats. Millinery as an industry, according to a study made in 1917, was a "disorganized, fluctuating, and seasonal occupation." Only 2.8 percent of milliners received pay for a full 52 weeks a year; only 7.6 percent for more than 48 weeks; 40 percent were on the payroll for four weeks or less each year. What this meant for many millinery workers was that job-hunting became necessary several times a year. The relatively high wages that experienced milliners earned during the brief busy seasons were eaten away by those periods without wages.

New York was the setting for the hat shop of Irene Molloy in the popular play by Thornton Wilder that began as *The Merchant of Yonkers*, became *The Matchmaker*, and was transformed into the hit musical *Hello, Dolly. The Merchant of Yonkers* depicts New York during the last part of the 19th century. Mrs. Molloy's comment that "all millineresses are suspected of being evil women" (although "the only men I ever get to meet are feather merchants") reflected a popular view of milliners. In a study of prostitution made by the resident physician at the Blackwell's Island Women's Prison in New York City and published in 1858, 41 of 2,000 prostitutes interviewed gave their previous occupation as milliner. This was perhaps more a result of the low pay, unemployment, and oversupply of workers in the field, however, than of any temptations found on the job in the form of feather merchants or others.

The use of feathers in women's hatmaking became a controversial issue at this time. By the 1890s public opinion was being aroused against the slaughter of birds in order to supply feathers for women's hats. In 1905 the National Audubon Society was organized to oppose the widespread destruction of bird life. The Audubon Society worked for the passage of the Audubon Plumage

Whole armies of people, including men, women, and children, were employed making artificial flowers, using punches of various designs to form the petals. (From Diderot's Encyclopedia, *late 18th century)*

Law, which prevented the slaughter of birds native to the United States and banned the importation or selling of osprey, bird of paradise, or feathers. Milliners were able to use dyed and cut goose and chicken feathers as substitutes.

An example of the poor conditions in the millinery industry can be found in the story of the *flower makers* who worked at home in the early 20th century. Flower makers were important suppliers to the millinery trade from the trade's origins. Their fortunes rose and fell with the fashion in the decoration of hats. Would it be feathers or flowers this year? The answer determined their fate.

Flower makers were generally women who worked at home, where they could mind their babies and the housework while they worked. A study published in 1913 tells of a family in a tenement on MacDougal Street in New York City. Seven family members lived and worked in three rooms. All except the father and two babies made violets. "The three-year-old picks apart the petals; her sister, aged four years, separates the stems, dipping an end of each into paste spread on a piece of board on the kitchen table and the mother and grandmother slip the petals up the stems." The family worked at this from 8 or 9 a.m. to 7 or 8 p.m., making perhaps 12 gross (one gross

= 144) of flowers per day for which they were paid 10 cents per gross. The rent they paid for their tenement was $10 per month.

This kind of repetitive work was more often found in the wholesale rather than the retail branch of the millinery industry. In the wholesale workroom each part of the hat was made by a separate group of workers. One worker might spend the day making dozens of hat linings, another concentrating on hat bands. This specialization was a point of concern to many of the workers. They envied the retail system in which milliners worked together in the making of one hat. This system increased their experience, thus enabling them to advance in the industry.

Millinery workers followed a strict hierarchy, especially in retail shops. The *designer* was on the highest rung of the ladder. She created the styles, often based on what she had viewed on her latest trip to Paris or London. *Millinery trimmers* (also known simply as milliners) used a variety of materials to interpret the ideas of the designers, usually sewing on the trimmings by hand. *Improvers* and *preparers* shirred chiffon, made folds, and put linings into hats. *Makers* constructed frames, covered them with crinoline and in other ways prepared hats for the trimmer. In many shops an informal apprenticeship system was used, under which inexperienced girls were hired to work as helpers at very low pay to aid the workers and thus gain experience.

In the early 20th century, labor unrest arose in the wholesale section of the millinery trade. Long hours, low wages, seasonal work, fines for the slightest errors, and the cost of their supplies and tools (which workers had to pay for themselves)—all these grievances pushed the workers into demanding better treatment from their employers. The women who made up the wholesale millinery industry were not easily moved to complain. Often recent immigrants who spoke little, if any, English, many of these women were happy to have even the smallest of incomes. But as they became more at home in the United States and saw other workers fight and win their battles for unionization, the women of the millinery trades began to speak out for their rights. In 1907 a Flower Maker's Union was organized in New York City although it lasted only about six months. A few years later factory workers tried to unite the milliners, wire makers, and flower makers into one union in order to control the trade, but the attempt failed.

In the late 1920s, efforts were strengthened to organize the women millinery workers. Male workers who were organized in the United Cloth Hat and Cap Makers' International Union received wages of $40 a week, worked 44 hours per week, and were paid time-and-a-half for overtime. The unorganized women milliners earned around $25 per week for unlimited hours with no overtime pay, no job security, and no rights of disagreement or appeal to their employers. These renewed attempts succeeded in organizing locals in Chicago, Boston, and a few other cities, as well as the very successful Millinery Hand Workers' Local 43 in New York City.

Local 43 was established with 400 women workers in 1924, and in just two years grew to 4,000 members, becoming the second largest local of women workers in the United States. The conservative faction of the United Cloth Hat and Cap Makers' International Union resented the growing strength of the largely radical Local 43. The conservatives of the International Union did everything in their power to dissolve Local 43, including gangster attacks on the women of the Local as they picketed outside their shops. One of Local 43's organizers was attacked and severely beaten in her own office; many other members were clubbed by police and imprisoned. By 1929, Local 43 had been effectively crushed and displaced by the less radical, though socialist, Millinery Local 24 in New York.

The drive toward complete unionization of the millinery industry continued during the 1930s. In 1932 the union called a stoppage in the industry in an attempt to unionize non-union shops. Because 35 of these shops were protected by racketeers, the union collected a volunteer force of 1,000 workers to protect the millinery district in New York from the gangsters hired by these shops. The stoppage succeeded in driving out the gangsters and unionizing the shops.

In the same year there was also a movement to combine the Cloth Hat, Cap, and Millinery Workers International Union (male and female workers in these areas had by then combined) with the United Hatters of North America. In 1934 the two unions merged to become the United Hatters, Cap and Millinery Workers International Union. There were 12 employers' organizations for millinery manufacturers, but not all manufacturers belonged to even one. More than one out of four firms were going out of business each year.

The unhealthy condition of the millinery industry was studied by the Department of Labor at the request of the Millinery Stabilization Board. The study, published in 1939, recommended better management of capital and expenditures in the industry and the lengthening of seasons for hats. Although some changes were made in the system based on this study, the millinery industry continued to fail. Imports from Italy, China, the Philippines, Central and South America, and Java flooded the market, at prices that undercut U.S. prices because of the cheap labor available in those other countries.

In the United States the successful completion of unionization within the millinery industry raised wages and cut the number of hours per week. Yet in 1959 there were only 37,100 workers in the hat, cap, and millinery trades, of whom less than a quarter were women. These workers earned average weekly wages of $61.90 for a 35- to 36-hour week. But the forces of fashion, automation, and cheap imports took their toll upon the millinery trade. The more casual fashions of the 1960s and 1970s ignored headgear for daily wear. The number of workers in the industry fell to under 16,000.

In recent decades milliners in both North America and Europe have suffered. France and Italy have lost some of their preeminence in high fashion, and all have been hard hit by the rise of more casual fashions. Hat shops, once commonplace, are rare today, and the stock of many hat departments is made by pieceworkers or factory workers in places such as the Philippines, Central and South America, and Java.

For related occupations in this volume, *Clothiers*, see the following:
Cloth Finishers
Fiber Workers
Hatters
Tailors and Dressmakers

For related occupations in other volumes of the series, see the following:
in *Financiers and Traders*:
Merchants and Shopkeepers
in *Manufacturers and Miners*:
Factory Workers
in *Warriors and Adventurers*:
Prostitutes

Shoemakers and Other Leatherworkers

A dented cone-shaped object, open at one end—perhaps a drinking cup—may be the earliest known object of leather. It dates from 7,000 years ago. Techniques for the preparation of leather were known to most of the oldest cultures. Fortunately, sand and dry soil have preserved Chinese, Central Asian, and Egyptian leather goods.

The first leather was stripped off already rotting animals. Only the center of the animal's hide is of use; hair and fat, two other layers, must be discarded. Primitive workers scraped these away with sharpened bones and rocks, both of which are common archaeological finds. The skin was submerged in dung as the first stage of *curing. Tanning* followed.

Different peoples used different materials and techniques to tan leather. In general the hide was immersed, through a drawn-out process, in baths of salt, alum, and *tannin*, a substance derived from bark and other vegetation, from which came the English word *tanning*. After being smoked over pits and then beaten smooth, the hide at last emerged as flexible but strong leather. It might be cut and sewn into clothing, yet made hard enough to repel sword cuts. Leather served as a perfect material for clothing during much of human history.

The nomads of the mountains, deserts, and steppes were exposed to harsh climates; they fashioned leather into boots. The ancient peoples around the Mediterranean lived in a warmer climate; they wore open leather sandals. In later societies in the north, the sandal gave way to closed shoes. But the first shoes and boots had almost been the same thing: simple flaps of hide with the animal's fur on the outside. Leather served only to make the thong that drew the shoe tight, like string wound around a bag to keep it closed.

The first professional *tanners* known to history worked 5,000 years ago among the Hittites, who lived in what is now Turkey. They experimented with alum and tannin, finding a mixture that produced the best leather of its time. Their rivals, the Egyptians, piled layers of hides four feet deep. Each layer was separated by crushed tannin pods; a pile of stones pressed down from the top. These would be left in place for years, while the damp skins absorbed and became permeated with the tannin. The result was soft leather, used for fancy cloaks and armbands. The Egyptians colored these black, red, yellow, or blue, using vegetable dyes. Rawhide was sometimes left half-tanned, for strength; it was laboriously sliced into thongs that held wheels to their carriages.

It is unclear whether the Egyptians made more of their sandals from papyrus or from leather. Papyrus sandals can still be found on mummies, 2,000 to 3,000 years after

Tanning was a messy business. After tanners removed skins from the ooze pit, they scraped and smoothed them. (By W.H. Pyne, from Picturesque Views of Rural Occupations in Early Nineteenth-century England, *1808)*

burial. The Greek historian Herodotus claimed that Egypt's priests chose to wear sandals of paper. These were made the same way as sheets of writing paper: Papyrus reeds were separated into flakes, dampened, molded together, and then left to dry in the sun. The finished paper sandals were worn with twisted leather thongs.

On the other hand, a Thebes wall painting, about 3,400 years old, shows two *sandal makers* at work. One uses an *awl*, a slender pointed rod, to punch holes in leather thongs. The other sews together a sandal's sole and its straps, meant to cross above the foot. The material is certainly leather. He works on a low bench with one end sloping to the ground for use as a cutting surface. A knife, for cutting out the parts of the sandal, is shaped in

Sandalmakers like these in Jerusalem have been at work in the East for over 3,000 years. (From Picturesque Palestine)

a semicircle, just like those used by shoemakers of the 19th century.

The Etruscans, a people of northern Italy who flourished over 500 years B.C., made the earliest *ankle shoes* (closed shoes). Etruscan sandals, with laces made from gold, became fashionable among wealthy Athenian women of the fifth century B.C. The Greek philosopher Socrates reproached Alcibiades, a proud political leader, for looking down on *shoemakers* and their trade. Shoemakers traditionally set up shop near the *agora*, an open marketplace where Socrates gathered with his friends. Socrates and Pericles, Athens' dictator, were said to visit with a shoemaker named Simon while he worked. Simon took a defiant pride in his craft, declaring in the midst of one debate, "I admit I am a shoemaker. No one is a better philosopher than Simon the shoemaker, and no one ever will be."

Kleon became one of Athens' joint rulers after the death of Pericles. He was a self-made man, and his enemies liked to remind the public that his fortune came from a tannery. Because they used large amounts of dung, the tanneries' smells made the trade a stock item

In this medieval shop, the shoemaker shows wares to a client, while the assistants keep on sewing. (From Frank Leslie's Popular Monthly Magazine*)*

for jokes. Aristophanes, the comic playwright, complimented Kleon on his "Heraclean bravery in braving the stenches of his trade." Heracles is better known today by his Roman name, Hercules. As one of his Twelve Labors, he had cleaned dung out of a monstrous stable, so the comparison is apt. Greek law demanded that tanners do their work on the outskirts of town. The people of Rome located their tanneries on the Tiber's west bank, safely away from the city.

Imperial Rome had at least 300 separate sandal makers' shops within the city. The Emperor Domitian, late in the first century A.D., had to order shoemakers off the streets because of the clutter caused by their goods. They turned out first-rate work in many styles. *Jewelers* added ornamentation to shoes for the very rich, but traders who sold their wares on public avenues must have made money from a considerably less affluent market.

Shoemakers appear in Christian legend as early saints of the church. The shoemaker St. Anianus of Alexandria was converted to Christianity by St. Mark himself, in the first century A.D. While repairing one of Mark's sandals, the shoemaker pricked himself with his awl and swore. Mark gave him a sermon about taking God's name in vain; then, in a miracle, he commanded the wound to vanish. Anianus eventually became a leader of the church, from 70 A.D. to his death in 86.

The story of St. Crispin and St. Crispianus is more grisly; it stayed a special favorite among shoemakers for many centuries. The brothers were noble, some said royal, Christians of the third century. Fleeing persecution of their sect, they escaped from Rome to Gaul (present-day France). Needing work to stay alive, they fell in among a company of shoemakers, somehow picking up enough skill to become the best in their trade. As Christians, they would work only for the poor, all the while gathering followers to the faith. Their success soon caught the emperor's attention. The brothers were found, arrested, and then put through terrible tortures. They survived a long line of these by divine intervention: as, when weighted with millstones, the two floated across the water. Boiling lead did nothing to them. At last, however, the miracles gave out and the brothers died, to become saints. Their day of canonization, October 25, was celebrated as a shoemaker's holiday through the 19th century.

In the East, the people of Japan made great use of leather. The warriors of northern Japan wore leather strong enough to serve as armor. Tanning was done simply by smoking buffalo hides at temperatures hot enough to make the skin shrink; the leather that resulted gave resistance to any blade. Legends told of the Empress Jingu, who went to war wearing leather armor painted with magic emblems. Imperial workshops of the first century A.D. were kept busy turning out leather bows and shields, though many of these were intended for sacrifice to the gods.

More advanced methods of treating leather traveled to Japan from China. Two Korean families carried further secrets to Japan in 493 A.D.; they fashioned the first

Fashionable clients did not frequent the shops; instead, shoemaker and assistant would bring their products into the home for inspection and selection. (Crispin and Crispianus, by W. Hollar, British Museum, early 17th century)

flexible leather to be found in the country. The finest Japanese leather was produced under the rule of the Kamakura clan, from 1185 to 1333 A.D. Leather softened by oil could be sewn into air-filled balls, for amusement at court. The Japanese mastered techniques that other nations could not match. *Japanese leather* was a type found only in that country: so pale as to be white, strong but easy to work. It was dyed in colors from yellow to purple, with many subtle shades. Japanese dyers used, as terms of their trade, such colors as "blue almost black" and "black as a crow."

The Japanese tanners washed hides in the Ishikawa River, whose waters were thought to have special properties. After being cleaned and cut to size, the hides were put back in the river again. The hairs then stripped off easily. The hides could be sliced into layers as thin as cloth. Women tanners poured on salt and river water, grinding these in with their feet. The hides were left for several days in the sun. The women then stamped in rapeseed oil obtained from a plant in the mustard family, and left the hides again to the open air. Each step was repeated. Workers cleaned the skins in the river, scrubbing them with sheaves of wheat straw. Piles of hides were stacked in place, sometimes for as long as a month. After this, the women went back to the beginning, repeating everything. In this way, an animal's hide could be beaten into leather of unique suppleness and strength.

Tanners of Europe's Middle Ages worked by curing, or *tawing*. Workers sliced off the flesh beneath a hide, then used a blunt blade to scrape away hairs; remains fell into a wooden trough called a *beam*. The hide was softened by rubbing in dung from dogs or chickens. Then the dung had to be cleaned away. The tanner dropped the hide in a bath of fermented bran. This was a rough process, and made for hard leather. But it could be carried on further, until a very supple material had been produced. The leather could be stretched over the beam to be worked over with a *currier's knife* (one held by two handles), then submerged again and again in solutions of tannin. At last, the leather would be left in a pit; as in ancient Egypt, bark separated each layer of skins. The skins stayed there for a year. (Techniques using hot water later compressed this to 10 days.) The leather did not come out as thin and fine as that of Japan, but it could be cut down and hand-fashioned for one use after another: scabbards, bellows, arm-bands, and, of course, shoes.

The first known piece of British leatherwork was the Stonyhurst Bible, handsomely bound with goatskin in 687 A.D. In later years, bindings of this sort could be richly ornamented. A volume of the period gives directions for gilding with gold leaf:

> To gild leather proceed as follows: take sheep leather as made by the tanner and soak it in clean water; strain it on a wooden frame as done for parchment and dry it well in the sun. To the dry leather apply the white of eggs and place the gold lead on top.

Tanners have always had a dirty job, soaking hides successively in water, lime, and tannin, and then drying them and scraping them. (By Jost Amman, from The Book of Trades, *late 16th century)*

Leather was versatile enough to serve as a luxury as well as a necessity. The *Ancren Riwle*, a book of domestic advice written some time between 1150 and 1230, gave as a maxim: "The dog that gnaws leather...men beat him immediately."

By the ninth century A.D., every monastery had its own clerical shoemakers, who made shoes for their fellow monks. Leatherworkers on the outside were most often women. Deer, sheep, and, less often, wolves provided hides. A man named Aelfric, a leatherworker of the 11th century, is almost alone among artisans of his era in setting down his thoughts on paper. He tells about his trade in the *Colloquies*:

> I buy hides and skins and I prepare them by my craft, and I make of them boots of various kinds, ankle-leathers, shoes, leather breeches, bottles, bridge-thongs, flasks and budgets, leather neckpieces, spur-leathers, halters, bags and pouches...

Most workers in leather were more specialized in choosing their trades than one might gather from Aelfric, who appears also to have been a tanner. By the 11th century, the London guilds of the *saddlers* and of the *botelers* (flask makers) were already well established and respected. There were at least seven other separate guilds that worked with leather. In 1422, the English catalogued every guild in the country; this time, the count of leather guilds came to 14.

Aelfric had remarked that "nobody would wish to go through winter without my craft." Leather artisans in truth did much of their work in clothing. In 1180 the London guild of girdlers—people who made *girdles*, which were wide bands encircling the waist—appears on the records; it was fined for organizing without a license. The London guild of *glovers*, or *gaunters*, ruled in 1349 that its workers could dye their goods; this had already become a popular custom.

Curriers scraped the tanned hides to prepare them for working into various items. (From Diderot's Encyclopedia, *late 18th century)*

A widespread use for leather, in Europe as in old Japan, was to make armor. The Saxons of England's Dark Ages worked leather into interlocking rings that shielded a warrior's tunic. This was called a *byrne*, and was known as early as the seventh century. From the 11th to the 13th centuries, *armorers* made great use of *cuir bouilli* which literally means "boiled leather." Since leather cannot actually be boiled, because water at that heat causes it to shrivel, no one knows how this leather could have been produced. One expert speculates that this may actually have been soft leather that had been molded and then blasted with heat to harden it; in short, it had been *fired*, like pottery.

A material that could be worked soft and then made hard might turn up as any item an armorer wanted to make. *Cuir bouilli* was made into helmets, shields, shinguards, even cups to fit over the knees. After the 13th century, the arms race of the Middle Ages replaced leather with impenetrable iron. A suit of armor's iron pieces still had to be held together, however, so leatherworkers turned to making strategic straps, called *points*, that acted as the armor's joints. An English ordinance of 1327 forbade the substitution of sheepskin for sturdier roebuck in points.

Shoes of the Dark Ages amounted to little more than bags slipped over the foot. Peasants wore shoes of plain

These leatherworkers are preparing a special kind of product called chamois. (From Diderot's Encyclopedia, *late 18th century)*

cattle hide, but the nobility, even at this time, could expect soft, specially treated leather. By the 11th century, work had become more complicated. A shoe was stitched horizontally, with upper and lower parts. The richest were of velvet or even silk, embroidered with gold. Fasteners—buckles, buttons, laces—gave a more secure fit.

The Moslem kingdom in what is now southern Spain exported boots made from a particularly fine red leather. The leather—named *cordewan* after their leather center of Cordoba—became the fashion for noble Europe. It also gave a new name to the shoemakers: in France, *cordonniers*; in England, *cordwainers*. England's cordwainer guilds passed ordinances against patching cordewan with lower-grade material. And cordwainers could not be seen near other leatherworkers at public fairs, where many of the raw materials of the time were bought and sold. The Cordwainers of Ghent, in the Netherlands, ratified their guild rules in 1304. France's King Charles V founded the Brotherhood of Companion Cordonniers in 1379, the ceremonies being held in the Cathedral of Paris.

Cordwainers clearly wanted to set themselves apart from other shoemakers. England's Henry VI granted a charter to the Cordwainers' Guild in 1439. They then petitioned him to ban the work of the *cobblers*. Cobblers sold secondhand shoes to the poorer classes, and earned rather an insecure living. Through the 18th century, some cobblers would wander from village to village, looking for repair work, ready to be dragged into any sort of job, as long as it paid. If the cobblers had the tools, they were willing. Cobblers often pulled teeth, before *dentists* penetrated the countryside; all it took was strength and a pair of pliers.

But cobblers used new leather to repair old shoes; this was what the cordwainers wanted to stop. Cordwainers and cobblers worked at different levels of skill for different levels of society, but they both made shoes. Apparently this was enough for their two trades to eventually merge. A Company of Shoemakers, which included both cobblers and cordwainers, was reported in York, England, in 1398.

All shoemakers, no matter what their guild, celebrated the day of St. Crispin and St. Crispianus. The holiday's heavy drinking became a stock item in the shoemakers' reputation. A traditional couplet runs, "On the twenty-fifth October/Ne'er a Souter's sober." *Souter* was a medieval term for shoemaker, taking in both cobblers and cordwainers.

The artisans who made shoes earned a good deal of both money and respect. The York Company of Shoemakers is first mentioned in public records because it was presented with a ceremonial silver bowl by an archbishop. A shoemaker of Troyes, France, was able to support his son in studies to join the clergy; that son became Pope Urban IV. The various guilds celebrated sacred days with public exhibitions of their prosperity. The shoemakers marched wearing armor and colorful uniforms; a man on horseback carried the guild's insignia printed on a banner.

Decoration of the best shoes had become rather elaborate. The Normans of late medieval France and England liked the effect of metal bands and studs; men especially enjoyed outdoing one another. The *cracowe* be-

Shoemakers made a wide variety of leather goods, including bags and cases, even holders for crossbows and water buckets for fighting fires. (By Jost Amman, from The Book of Trades, *late 16th century)*

came popular; its thin pointed toe would reach as long as the wearer's money would permit it; 30 inches was the record. However, nobles wore these only indoors, when on display; outside, rough weather required them to wear wooden clogs.

The English Parliment of 1463 set new laws for the shoemaker's work. *Beakes* (projecting points on shoes) could extend no more than two inches. Violation meant cursing by a priest and paying a fine: one-third to London's city government, one-third to the throne, one-third to the guild. The same penalties applied to working on Sundays. Wardens of the Cordwainers' Guild enforced the rules.

Buff, a thick soft, undyed leather originally used for a light armor tunic, could also be found in civilian jackets and hats by the 16th century. Spanish leatherworkers, who specialized in this kind of leather, exported goods all over Europe. Spain's cattle could not satisfy the booming trade in its cities, however, so more leather came from sparsely populated nations that could support greater herds. Shipments of hides from North Africa, imported by Italy's merchants for use by Spanish artisans, spurred Islamic-European trade. By midway through the 16th century, the merchants were seeking hides from greater and greater distances. Poland and Russia filled the demand for a while, but at last Europe turned to the newly discovered Americas. By 1608, Dutch ships were carrying hides out of the Caribbean.

Gradually, the leatherworker's craft grew more subtle. Boots became sturdier, and the ornamentation of shoes, now generally reserved for the female trade, primarily involved intricate stitching of brocade and embroidery. Shoemakers and their workshops could be found in every good-sized town of England and France.

An Elizabethan comedy, *The Shoe-makers' Holyday—or the Gentle Craft*, written in 16th century-England, was based on the career of Sir Simon Eyre. He had been both a shoemaker and a very good businessman; his talents turned him into one of London's financial powers, and, in time, a member of the nobility.

The lastmaker was a specialist who made wooden models of the customer's feet, so the shoes might be fitted perfectly. (From Diderot's Encyclopedia, *late 18th century)*

As a character in the play, Eyre boasts happily, "Prince am I none, yet I am nobly born, as being the sole son of a shoemaker." The play was dedicated "To all good Fellowes, Professors [practitioners] of the Gentle Craft: of what degree soever." The Queen demanded a New Year's night performance. "The gentle craft" had been given as shoemaking's name, so tradition claimed, after England's Edward IV had spent the night drinking with a party of cobblers.

One speech of *The Shoe-makers' Holy-day* runs down a list of the tools of the trade; "your four sorts of awls, your two balls of wax, your paring knife, your hand and thumb leathers [for protection], and good St. Hugh's bones [used to work the leather] to smooth up your work..."

Shoemakers' guilds in Germany required apprenticeships of three years. The apprentice had to be entirely German in blood, his parents married at his birth, and with no sort of trouble with the law in his past. His time as a journeyman, spent wandering for work and experience from town to town, might stretch out to seven years. He could graduate to the rank of *master* and open his own shop only upon return to the town of his birth. He dressed simply in his workshop, wearing breeches, a narrow apron, and a shirt without a jacket.

Simon Eyre, speaking in the *The Shoe-maker's Holy-day*, had said he would take no work from the lower classes. He advised his apprentices where money for the trade could be found: "Ladies of the court, fine ladies, my lads, commit their feet to our apparelling." In England during the late 17th century, some shoemakers specialized in making shoes for the fashionable members of the aristocracy. They produced custom-made shoes according to individual specifications of ornament and material. The trade had divided somewhat into footwear for men and footwear for women. Men wore shoes of black leather; the more sporting adopted red heels. Women preferred their shoes made from silk, embroidered with florid patterns of flowers and leaves.

A poem circulated at the court of Louis XIV of France was inspired by a shoemaker named Nicholas Lestage: "Let no one blame the trade/By whom our shoes are made/For you have made it noble." Lestage had presented a pair of boots to his king; their quality made them a universal wonder. These lines came from a book of poems on the event, published in 1677. Twenty men had worked under Lestage in Bordeaux, where he was already a man of substance. After this he became shoemaker to the King. The Paris guild of shoemakers received him as a hero, and his portrait was hung in the king's gallery. To top himself, in 1663 Lestage molded a seamless boot made entirely from one piece of leather. His colleagues were baffled; another poem of the day announced "man is not its inventor." This left the chance of supernatural aid, in the 17th century still thought a possibility. Lestage fled Paris. His seamless boot was never seen again. Samuel Campion, a Victorian chronicler of the shoemakers, wrote of Lestage as "the miracle of his age: after the boot he made, mind and art could no further go."

A rich trade went on in leather and leather goods, rich enough for 18th-century tanners to compete in finding new and finer leathers—rich enough for the methods they used to stay secret. By this time even the working classes of London had become so accustomed to leather shoes that public riots broke out after Robert Walpole, the government's leader, placed an excise tax on their import.

Upper-class women expected their shoes to sport bows, laces, and gold leaf, although they still wore clogs for walking outside. Shoes were not fitted to the exact contours of the foot. The shoemaker noted the length of his client's foot very precisely. He used a "size stick," a pole with a sliding upright stop. It was like the measuring tools used in shoe stores today, except that it did not allow for making the width or shape of the customer's foot. Length was what counted, and everything else was

These Peking shoemakers are making shoes much as their forebears had done for thousands of years. (From G. Waldo Browne's The New America and the Far East, *1901)*

taken care of by calling a foot small, medium, or large. Shoes were made straight, with no distinction between the right foot and the left.

The shoemakers of the 18th century produced more than a trade's fair share of both successes and eccentrics. James Lackington, a shoemaker born in 1740, died rich—in spite of his hobby of paying for buildings, including a "Temple of the Muses" and at least one Wesleyan chapel that cost him £2,000 (around $25,000 today). Late in the century, a cobbler named Thomas Hardy launched a campaign for reform of Parliament; he went to jail, briefly. This streak of rebellion persisted. Shoemakers led the Cato Street Conspiracy of the 1820s, a plot to assassinate all of England's Cabinet. As late as the 1840s, Sir Robert Peel, after meeting a group of artisans with two cobblers as spokesmen, remarked that shoemakers were always at the heart of every working-class agitation. Samuel Campion, defender of the trade, noted that "Taken broadly, this was really an indirect compliment." Peel perhaps appreciated independence of mind, Campion suggested.

Campion was worried by what others thought of his trade. He wrote in 1874 that, "Somehow or other the trade of a shoemaker had been looked down upon with some degree of contempt." Shoemakers were often thoughtful and talented people, but when they proved this by changing careers, others might seek to remind them of their past. Byron, a famous 19th-century British poet, reminded three rivals of their origin with a compliment that, at best, seems ambiguous:

Ye tuneful cobblers, still your notes prolong,
Compose at once a slipper and a song.
So shall the fair your handiwork reuse,
Your sonnets sure shall please,
Perhaps your shoes.

Playwright Richard Sheridan was also a Member of Parliament representing the city of Stafford (which, along with Northampton, was one of England's shoemaking centers). At a political banquet, Sheridan exercised his wit upon his constituents, offering as a toast: "May the staple trade of Stafford be trodden underfoot by the whole world." Stafford and Northampton produced shoes for sale all over the nation. In centers like these, in England and elsewhere, many independent artisans were being collected into larger work teams, their jobs divided among more and more anonymous hands. Tanners generally concentrated their works first; then shoemakers set up shop nearby for the leather.

The city of Lynn, in Massachusetts, became a shoemakers' center because the first tannery of the North American Colonies was built there, in 1630. This came before the first guild of American shoemakers, chartered in Boston in 1648. With the leather left over from individual commissions, shoemakers began making shoes

Cobblers serving the poor, like this one from Japan, often sat by the side of the road to do shoe repairs. (From G. Waldo Browne's The New America and the Far East, *1901)*

for display in their shop windows hoping to attract more customers. The American shoemakers gradually gathered into larger and larger establishments. No longer were they occupied primarily in work that had been ordered by clients. Instead, teams of workers turned out shoes by routine, and customers bought what pleased them. By 1767, John Dagyr's manufactory in Lynn, the biggest shoe workshop in the Colonies, was making 80,000 pairs of shoes in a year.

With the coming of industrialization, a variety of revolving blades took over much of the tanner's work. They did away with hair and flesh, reducing a hide to its usable central skin. The *splitting machine* of the early 19th century shaved hides more closely and more quickly than the tanner had ever done with a currier's knife. The *band-knife splitter* sliced the leather into precise layers.

Meanwhile the number of shoemakers in London rose 30 percent through the 1830s, while population had risen 10 percent. In 1841, the journalist Henry Mayhew counted 18,574 shoemakers and bootmakers in London; by comparison, there were 6,000 *bricklayers*. Mayhew's

In modern times, cobblers came to work at benches in shops owned by others, often simply making repairs on factory-made shoes. (From Harper's New Monthly Magazine)

figures are not exact; but he was a master *journalist*, and the reports he made on the Victorian working classes at least show general proportions. He calculated that 2,000 of the 18,574 were *master bootmakers*, highly skilled artisans who were the employers or supervisors of the other workers.

Shoemakers of London's East End sweated in the factories, turning out routine work, with supervisors periodically stepping up the pace of production. Shoemakers in the more prosperous West End remained independent craftspeople; profits came from serving the well-to-do. One West End bootmaker reported that he worked part-time at "the best shop"; the rest of the time he got by on odd jobs, or "by-strokes." He would stay working all week with his wife and an apprentice to help him. "In the course of last season" this earned him just £3 a week. Without wife and apprentice, he would have had to work 14 hours a day to even approach that weekly figure.

The factories of Northampton and the East End had forced cutthroat competition; Mayhew estimated the drop in earnings in one decade, 1840 to 1850, to be roughly a fifth. The best of the master shoemakers made money; income for everybody else in their trade was declining. Workers gravitated toward work in one of the factories.

Lobb's, leader of West End boot shops in the 19th century, gives a demonstration of how shoemakers had traditionally worked. The *clicker* ran the show, just as he did in the factories; but here he led a handful of artisans, no more than 10, rather than a laborers' squadron. The clicker's knife was tiny but kept fearfully sharp; it sliced out from leather the separate pieces that made up a boot's *upper*. For Lobb's, eight was the minimum. Custom-made work demanded that the clickers shape each piece to match the contours of the client's feet. A *closer* sewed the segments together. Then the upper was fitted for molding over the *last*, a wood model of the customer's foot. Adding on the sole and heel took two days. The leather of the inner sole had to be submerged in water to be made soft and yielding; then it was stretched along the last's base. These lower pieces had been fashioned by a counterpart to the clicker, his hands requiring not quite so delicate a touch. The upper's border was folded into a lip, then stitched to the sole. Artisans calculated the number of stitches by the leather's strength, and by the weight and stance of the wearer-to-be. The heel came last. A shoe or boot with every piece in place still had to be polished. Waxed calf leather took hours of work; liquid blacking was rubbed in with a bone, preferably deer bone.

The workers at Lobb's spent, on the average, four months to finish each pair of boots they made. The market they worked for paid well. But the typical cobbler, in 1856, spent 1,025 hours to make 100 pairs of shoes for women. His labor costs came to $256.33, and his customers would never reward him nearly so well as those of Lobb's. An American factory in 1895 could make the same number of shoes at a labor cost of $18.59. United States exports frightened foreign producers into change.

The census of 1907 found three-quarters of all British shoemakers were workers in fully industrialized factories, tending to machines and doing little more. The factories were small, but they could swamp the artisans remaining on the outside. By this time factories were producing almost 90 percent of British shoes. During World War I, the factories of Northampton furnished 23,000,000 pairs of military boots for the emergency.

In tanning, rapidly spinning drums began to transform hides in a fraction of the time once required by soaking in pits. Tanning was still smelly, unattractive work, but immigrants from poorer countries were glad to take jobs others shunned. August Schultz, working in America, developed the *chrome method* of treating leather. Producing innovations in leather-dyeing and preparation became one of chemistry's more profitable branches, for a new variety of leathers could be made from familiar hides. By about 1910, the American *yellow boot*, called in England the *bulldog*, caught on, not just with the upper classes, but with the lower as well. In-

Most modern leatherworkers are employed in factories; these are putting soles on shoes at the B.F. Spinney Company of Lynn, Massachusetts. (Authors' archives)

dustrialism had at last created a style that those below the wealthy could afford.

Lobb's of London still sells its boots, and the boots, as before, are made by hand at high prices. Writer Max Beerbohm, on his deathbed in 1956, asked a visiting journalist, "Tell me, is Lobb still the best bootmaker in London?" The London workshop employs no more than the traditional 10 men, although outside London others work alone in homes across Great Britain, sending their finished product to headquarters. Lobb's still makes the finest boots, but it has also become the only employer left for anyone who wishes to make boots the old-fashioned way.

The pattern is the same the world over, as the work once done by tanners, shoemakers, and other leatherworkers is largely done by machine, except for the occasional fine artisan working for a select clientele. If many small towns still have cobblers, it is only because they have a trade in repairing damaged or worn shoes, or in modifying shoes for people with foot problems.

For related occupations in this volume, *Clothiers*, see the following:
 Cloth Finishers
 Tailors and Dressmakers

For related occupations in other volumes of the series, see the following:
in *Artists and Artisans:*
 Bookbinders
 Jewelers
in *Communicators*
 Printers
in *Financiers and Traders*:
 Merchants and Shopkeepers
in *Healers:*
 Dentists
in *Manufacturers and Miners:*
 Weapon makers

Spinners

Spinning is the process of turning fibers into yarn. It has traditionally been the responsibility of the women in a household to spin. Recognition of this responsibility carried over into our language: A *spinster* became the legal designation for a never-married woman, and the phrase "on the *distaff* side" (another weaving term explained below) refers to the mother's side of the family.

The earliest yarn was probably made by rolling the fibers between the palms of one's hands or along the thigh. But it was the *spindle*—the basic device used in making yarn—that became one of the oldest tools known to human beings. The spindle is a stick that holds the yarn while it is being spun. Fastened to the spindle is a *whorl*, doughnut-shaped disk that helps keep the spindle rotating and also keeps the spun yarn on the spindle. Rotating the spindle twists the fibers together to produce a strand of yarn. The *distaff* is the stick that holds the fibers that are spun. Clay or stone spindle whorls have been found in archaeological excavations of the Swiss lakes. The Swiss Lake Dwellers who inhabited the area before 8000 B.C. used these tools to spin wool and flax into thread for baskets, nets, and probably crude clothing.

One advantage of the spindle is that it is easily portable and, although spinning demands some manual dexterity, it is a task that can be accomplished when one's attention is elsewhere. Women with responsibility for running a household and taking care of children could do their spinning and attend to other important matters at the same time. Spinning was carried on in roughly the same way through biblical and Classical times. As late as the Middle Ages a familiar sight would be women with distaffs tucked under one arm, busily twirling their spindles, while simultaneously out in the fields minding sheep.

Using the basic spindle that would be in use for centuries, these Egyptian women are preparing yarn to be used on the vertical loom at lower left. (From Clara Erskine Clement's Egypt, *1903)*

Around 750 A.D. the *spinning wheel* was invented in India; the spindle was mounted on a frame and rotated by turning a wheel attached to the spindle by a cord. This tool was not much faster than the spindle alone, but it did turn out a yarn that was smoother and more uniform. Its disadvantage was that the spinning wheel was not as portable as the distaff and spindle, so both tools were often used, at different times, by the same spinners. This spinning wheel, later known as the *Jersey wheel*, was probably introduced to Northern Europe during the 13th century.

Spinning during the Middle Ages was definitely women's work. The patron saint of spinning was St. Catherine, because she was tortured and killed while tied to a giant wheel. (The modern firework known as the catherine wheel, which spins off into the sky in a blaze of sparks, is named after this saint.) The great households of this time had serfs who would prepare yarn for weaving the materials needed, but even noblewomen would

In countless tales and legends, young women were set to spinning—hence, the name spinster. *(From* Art of the Book*)*

be familiar with the spinning process. It was said that the Emperor Charlemagne preferred that his clothing be made of homespun materials—to keep his daughters busy and out of mischief. Spinning was a cottage industry, done in the home to supply household and local weavers with yarn. It took four to six spinners to provide enough yarn to keep a handloom *weaver* occupied.

The spinning wheel was improved—some say by Leonardo da Vinci—by the addition of the *flyer*, a U-shaped device that enabled the yarn to be wound on the spindle as the wheel was turning the spindle to twist the fiber. In Paris, though not in England, spinners formed a guild to organize their craft.

Spinning wheels were among the essential tools that were brought to America by the earliest settlers. Spinning was one of the chief occupations of women in the American Colonies, and a wheel could be found in every home. During the period before the Revolutionary War, Colonial women formed a group known as the Daughters of Liberty, the "distaff side" of the Sons of Liberty. They organized boycotts against English products such as tea and textiles. The Daughters of Liberty devoted themselves to making American textiles by spinning and weaving, responding to an appeal addressed to them that read:

First then throw aside your high top knots of pride
Wear none but your own country linen.
Of economy boast. Let your pride be the most
To show cloaths of your own make and spinning.

Spinning bees or contests were organized among the Daughters of Liberty in Boston, setting records for the amount of yarn spun.

The cottage industry of spinning continued for centuries around the world. Spinning was one of those domestic tasks that was seen as inseparable from other aspects of good housewifery. In time, the domestic, or *putting-out,* system developed, in which women would spin at home in order to supply weavers who were not of their household, using materials supplied by *clothiers.* The wool would be delivered to the spinner by weight and, when she returned it, it would again be weighed. During the early 17th century expert spinners might earn a shilling a day, and children, who were taught to spin at an early age, could earn from sixpence to one shilling and sixpence a week. As in earlier times, four to six spinners worked to supply threads for each weaver.

About this time new tools were invented that enabled women to spin yarn much faster than ever before. There was much resistance to such innovation in the textile industry. Weavers in particular were vehement and destructive in their protests against machinery. Weavers had a tradition and a guild organization that made their opposition a force to be reckoned with. In addition, weaving could proceed only as fast as the supply of yarn would let it. So the inventors focused on mechanizing the process of spinning.

In 1767 James Hargreaves, a poor and uneducated English spinner, invented the *spinning jenny.* The jenny is a frame that holds two racks of spindles, which are connected and can increase the amount of yarn being spun at one time. Hargreaves's invention was not well received—he ended up dying on a poor farm—but the

A variety of devices were later developed to be used in spinning. (From Diderot's Encyclopedia, *late 18th century)*

principle behind his invention helped Richard Arkwright invent a waterpowered spinning machine. While the jenny was small enough to be used in the home, Arkwright's invention required more space and a water supply. By 1782 he had opened factories in England that employed 5,000 people to run these water frames. In 1779 Samuel Crompton carried the principle Arkwright had used even further and invented the cotton *mule,* a device that could make fine yarn even more quickly because one spinner could watch over 1,000 spindles at the same time.

Moving the process of spinning from the cottage to the factories—or *mills* as they were known—created enormous changes in society. No longer were families able to work together to make a piece of cloth. Industrial innovation required specialization of parts of the process; mass production robbed the individual of pride in craftsmanship. But the strain on society was seen more in the employment of women and children in the mills. Accustomed in the past to working at their own speed with time out for household chores, childcare, and neighborliness, the new workers were forced to keep pace with the new machines, which worked at inhuman speeds for inhuman lengths of time. The machine owners, in order to make the most of their capital investments, preferred to keep the machines working around the clock, causing the new worker to work long shifts in cold and darkness.

The outrages of England's "satanic mills" became well known over the years. Eventually much was done—by government, the mill owners, and the workers themselves—to solve or try to solve some of the problems associated with industrialization. But many of these social problems are still with us.

In the United States textiles became a thriving industry, especially after Eli Whitney's invention in 1793 of the *cotton gin,* a machine that increased the rate at which cotton could be separated from its seed. By the War of 1812 there were 169 small spinning and weaving plants near Providence, Rhode Island. One of the most famous

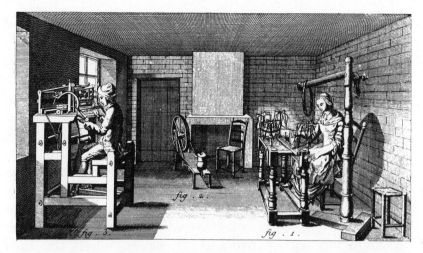

Before the age of factories, spinners often worked alongside weavers in small, private quarters. (From Diderot's Encyclopedia, *late 18th century)*

of the early cotton mills was in Lowell, Massachusetts. In 1834 the Lowell mills employed 6,000 workers, known as *operatives*. Of these, nearly 5,000 were girls between the ages of 17 and 24. Most of these girls were farmers' daughters from New England, who were happy to experience life off the farm for a few years and to save up money for when they would marry. The Lowell management, knowing that New England farmers would not let their daughters travel and work at a place touched by scandal or any hint of immorality, built dormitories for the young women, hired matrons, and saw to it that the workers' lives were above reproach. There was little time for these women to get into trouble, in any case, for the average work week extended to 70 hours.

Not every mill showed such a fatherly interest in its employees, however, and conditions could be quite oppressive. In many mills six-year-old children worked at spinning machines. Whole families would spend their days working in separate areas in the mills. A report made in Boston in 1832 stated that two-fifths of the workers in the textile mills were children between the ages of six and seventeen. Even the best-run mills held health hazards. The air would be filled with flying bits of cotton, which would enter the nostrils, throats, and lungs of the workers. Pneumonia, consumption, tuberculosis, and other lung diseases were familiar cripplers and killers in the villages that surrounded the mills.

Many attempts were made by the employees of the mills to organize and demand their rights. In 1845 the Lowell Female Labor Reform Association was formed in the mill towns of Massachusetts. The Female Labor Reform Association pledged to work for the 10-hour day and improvements in the sanitary and lighting conditions in the mills. In 1874 spinners and weavers working in Fall River, Massachusetts, formed a Weavers' Protective Association. Members of the Association went on strike when pay cuts were made in 1874 and 1875. The Association was wiped out, however, when the mill management blacklisted its leaders, that is, fired them and made it impossible for them to get employment anywhere else in the industry. Pay cuts in the mills mounted up to 40 percent in 1875.

During the late 19th century and well into the 20th, the shift in textile production in the United States was from the mill towns of New England to the South. In 1896 the Lowell Mills closed. The South provided the mill owners with cheap, unorganized labor. The mill owners considered Southerners to be unorganizable because they had not been influenced by "foreign" socialist ideas, as had the immigrant mill workers of the North. The American Federation of Labor (known as the AFL), along with the National Union of Textile Workers, continued its

These ropemakers are working outdoors, but many of their colleagues worked in long indoor ropewalks. (By W.H. Pyne, from Picturesque Views of Rural Occupations in Early Nineteenth-century England, *1808)*

attempts to organize mill workers in the South as well as the North. The workers organized, and the strikes spread through the mill towns of Tennessee and North Carolina. These strikes, which met with limited success, were the forerunners of the great labor struggles of the 1930s which led to the founding of the Congress of Industrial Organizations (known as the CIO).

One craft closely related to spinning is rope making. Rope is one of the few objects made by spinning yet not meant to be worn. *Rope makers*, working by hand, labored in every tropical nation where fiber-bearing plants grew. First a palm leaf had to be stripped. Then the rope maker twined two of its fibers by rolling them across his thigh. Two of these double-fibered strands were then twined together in the same way. The worker continued until he had a rope of satisfactory strength.

The spinning wheel could twine the fibers far faster, however. In Europe from the end of the Middle Ages to the 19th century, it was the practice for a boy apprentice to keep the wheel turning, while his master stepped slowly backwards, a heap of fibers from the hemp plant in his arms. The hemp whirred through the wheel, the master judging its progress into rope as he let out more fiber. *Rope walks*, which provided room for the rope to be stretched out in lengths, were especially common in seaport towns, where ships being fitted out for sea needed long, strong rope for their rigging.

As many medieval women were kept busy spinning, this monk is occupied making rope. (By Albrecht Dürer, early 16th century)

Factories today twirl rope around fiber cores. A thin fiber is strung through the stranding machine; the machine then winds metal wires around it. This makes a strand. A second machine, a larger edition of the first, winds these strands into a wire-rope, again using a thin rope as a core. The larger the core, the more easily the rope bends. Like the spinner, the rope maker has largely been replaced by the factory worker tending huge machines.

For related occupations in this volume, *Clothiers*, see the following:
    Cloth Finishers
    Fiber Workers
    Weavers

For related occupations in other volumes of the series, see the following:
in *Manufacturers and Miners*
    Factory Workers

Tailors and Dressmakers

Tailors and dressmakers—people who sew together garments from separate pieces of cloth—have practiced in relatively few nations through history. In the ancient kingdoms of the Middle East, such as Egypt and Assyria, people wore loose-fitting tunics, skirts, girdles, mantles, and robes—each item in a single piece, woven or cut whole. Modern civilization in Europe and North America has borrowed a great deal from the civilization of the ancient Greeks, but not its style of dress. The ancient world's clothing was wound or draped about the body; nothing was sewn or made so that the body had to fit into it.

People who shape clothes by sewing hardly figure in most of the world. For centuries, Japanese sewing was counted as one of the minor accessory crafts used in

81

preparing clothes. Sewers for the emperor and his court were included with miscellaneous other clothing workers under the Bureau of the Palace Wardrobe in the Ministry for Central Affairs. The people of India designed their clothing so that it hung in as close to a straight line as possible. It was meant to do nothing but keep the body from sight. Having done this, the clothing itself was meant to be ignored. Long before the Christian era, Indian writers listed 18 sciences and 64 arts that their people had mastered, including the arrangement of flowers on one's person. But sewing and tailoring were not listed.

Tailored clothing first appeared outside the ancient civilizations—perhaps about 2000 B.C. Nomads of Central Asia began to sew together animal hides to form trousers and jackets. These gave covering and heat without wrapping around the limbs. The people who lived along the steppes and among the mountains had to be able to move quickly and with freedom. Their southern rivals, the Persians, seem to have been the only civilized peoples of the ancient world to employ tailors (by about seventh century B.C.) A portrait from the fifth century B.C. shows a Persian shah wearing a pair of pants. For centuries, this sort of clothing, tailored to fit the limbs and always practical, could be found only in the wastes of Central Asia and along its outskirts: in Persia, in the northern provinces of India, and, among commoners and soldiers, in northern China.

Tailors and dressmakers have done most of their work in the West, beginning in medieval Europe. During the Dark Ages, from the Roman Empire's fall in the fifth century A.D. to the ninth century, women generally prepared clothing. This was not done for pay; a peasant's wife or the lady of a manor made her household's clothes as a domestic duty. Having woven the cloth, these women sewed together the clothing, acting as *seamstresses*, women who sew clothes.

It took some centuries for men to take up the craft and make a living by it. These men were called, in a term

Before the days of machines and factories, hosiery was made by hand, as by this Chinese needleworker. (From G. Waldo Browne's The New America and the Far East, *1901)*

taken from the Latin language of Rome, *cissorii*, or *cissors*. The domestic seamstress made clothing meant for the home. The cissors specialized in formal wear, serving both men and women. In the family of England's Edward I (who ruled from 1272-1307), each member employed a cissor.

As the trade grew, cissors', or tailors', guilds appeared. Henry I of England granted a royal charter to the Taylors of Oxford in 1100. In 1299, the London Guild of Taylors and Linen Armorers was awarded a coat of arms. *Linen armorers* provided padding for noblemen's chainmail protective gear. Even in a city as rich as London, the tailors saw no need to separate themselves from linen armorers until 1466.

In an age when most people made their own clothes, the tailor (schneider) worked primarily for the upper classes, making fine clothes and tents and flags. (By Jost Amman, from The Book of Trades, *late 16th century)*

The French throne chartered the Paris *Tailleurs de Robe* (Clothing Tailors) in 1293. The French sewers of hose, a medieval item something like a combination of pants and stockings, founded their own guild in 1346. Further guilds of tailors, each guarding its own specialty, followed. They did not combine until 1588 with the founding of the joint guild of the Master Clothing Tailors.

A few English women, at least, were able to work at this trade outside of the home. The city of Oxford listed the occupations of its inhabitants in the 1380 tax rolls. Eleven women worked as *shapesters*, another term for tailors. The town of West Riding, in 1379, listed 22 seamstresses. (By comparison, 39 women worked as *brewers*.)

Tailors sew, but the pieces that they sew together must be precisely cut if the finished garment is to be any good. From the Middle Ages on, tailors have relied on *patterns*, paper outlines used as guides in cutting out cloth. People

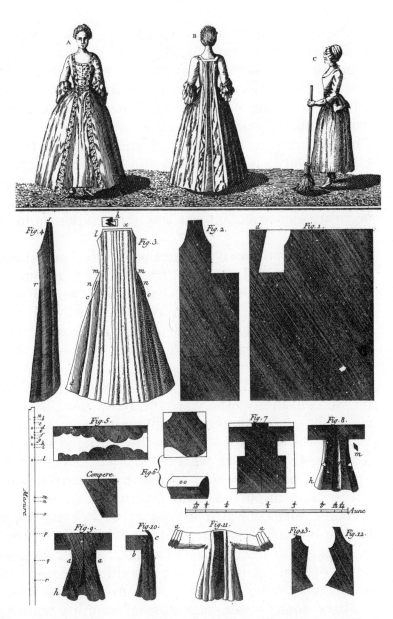

Patterns were an important part of a tailor's or dressmaker's assets. (From Diderot's Encyclopedia, late 18th century)

could not make a living as tailors unless the patterns they had collected matched a wide variety of human measurements. Young apprentices often demanded copies of their masters' patterns as part of the agreed-upon terms of their apprenticeship. Some tailors refused, instead handling their stock down from generation to generation as family secrets.

The first known book on tailoring was published in 1589; translated from the Spanish, its title is *Book of Practical Geometry in Tailoring*. How much cloth does one need for different items of clothing? "The tailor who wished to cut his clothes well, either for a man or for a woman, should take careful measurements of his clients." The author warned that one should never trust the client's word; people either did not know their own figures, or else were in the habit of lying whenever the subject came up. Along with precise cutting, quick and accurate measurement was a skill the tailor could not do without.

With Europe's revival after the Middle Ages, the clothing crafts multiplied. From the 16th century on, many people, not just kings and great lords, expected not only mere covering but also distinction from what they wore. A tailor's measurement and cutting came to be important because customers expected a great deal from the look and fit of their clothing.

Many tailors still made suits for men and also dresses for women; many others, virtually all men, worked exclusively as *dressmakers*. Fashionable women competed both in the number of gowns they ordered and in how lavishly the dresses were decorated. Then *milliners* appeared on the scene, managing expensive London shops that imported from Milan the fans, feathers, ribbons, laces, brooches, and other "pretty toies for Gentlewomen" that were in great demand.

Taking milliners as their models, seamstresses set up shops of their own, making ruffs (high pleated collars) and shirts for both sexes. Young girls of the late 17th century spent seven-year apprenticeships training as seamstresses. A writer of the time tells us that:

Seamster or Seamstry work follows next in order to adorn the Head, Hands, and Feet, as the other [the tailor] is for the covering of the body; nay, very often the Seamster occupieth the room and place of a Taylor in furnishing the Nobility and Gentry with such conveniences as serve the whole body, especially in the Summer Season....

The seamstresses of France, petitioning the throne in 1675, were the first to win the right to fashion women's dresses, once the province of master tailors. Seamstresses also specialized in making nightgowns and underclothes, for both women and small children.

Tailors, dressmakers, and seamstresses could make enviable livings. A popular English compendium called *A General Description of all Trades*, published in 1747, told in its entry on "Taylors" that it:

...took strength and skill to make good wages at it [tailoring] which most of them do...Some Masters carry a great business indeed, many of them in a middling Way live exceedingly handsome, and the honest Class of them that are frugal get a good livelihood, and some of the first sort have left Estates behind them.

After taking measurements, recorded on a parchment strip, the tailor chose from the shop's private collection the paper pattern that came most precisely to the customer's size, and traced this in chalk on the fabric the client had picked out. Then, reading the measurements and relying on a mental record of the client's needs, the tailor adjusted the outline to satisfaction, folded the fabric over, and cut along the chalk lines to produce both sides of the garment.

This shell was first filled-out with a sewn lining, and then stitched together at the seams. Pressing stiffened the garment, sealing its seams and giving it shape; the tailor used a specially-made iron, called a *goose*, weighing from 16 to 25 pounds. Apprentices kept check on the goose as it warmed over the workroom fire, but only a master tailor would be trusted to use it, because if it was

In an age when heating was sparse and largely ineffective, the furrier was a most favored specialized tailor. (By Jost Amman, from The Book of Trades, *late 16th century)*

not used carefully, the goose could scorch through a thick pile of fabric. Tailors worked with common thread and needles, but their *shears* were of special weight. In most catalogues, "Taylors shears" appeared as an item apart from "Women's Sizzars." Learning to use the goose and shears competently, as well as to sew with the skill demanded by the trade, took years of practice.

Measurement, a skill of mind and eye, set the best tailors above their colleagues. A suit was meant for one man only; it presented him to the world. If he had any claim to living in good society, his suit had to make that claim known. The tailor prepared his client to step forward and take a place among his peers. A suit was meant not just to cover its wearer; it transformed him, giving his frame and bearing more poise than it might

Precise measurements were the key to success in tailoring. (From Diderot's Encyclopedia, *late 18th century)*

naturally have. A tailor took it as his job, one authority wrote, "To bestow a good shape where Nature has not designed it."

The tailor made a study of his client once the man had stepped into his workroom, "not only the shape but the common Gait of the Subject." The suit was designed, with the precision that would go into a watch, to take account of and overcome each curve, stoop, stretch, and twist in a man's body. A good tailor kept a file of his clients' measurements—neck size, arm length, breadth of the thigh, and so on—notched on his strip of parchment in a code that only he could read. Cutting out the suit's components, and then pressing them so that they kept the proper shape once sewn together, were considered the most demanding of the tailor's hand-skills.

The man of fashion counted his suit as a major investment, in somewhat the same way as the average consumer of today regards a new car. In England's North American Colonies, those who could afford it sent their money, for both fabric and skilled workmanship, across the sea to a London tailor; they would mail their measurements, or, if possible, go to London themselves for a personal examination. Dress revealed a person's status in society. A gentleman could disguise himself as a farmer or workman, one of the "meaner sort," simply by wearing cheap, poorly made trousers. Some well-born

Americans did just that in the 1765 riot against the Stamp Act.

A good tailor worked for those who could claim a high position in society. He relied for a living on the rich, serving a circle so small that customers could be treated as patrons. Two American tailors, Egan and M'Danell, were proud to announce in the newspapers that their new partnership was formed after "being greatly encouraged by many Gentlemen of the first rank in this city..." They wanted to "inform the public, and their friends in particular, that they purpose carrying on the business extensively in its several branches, suitable both for Gentlemen and Ladies..."

For "Ladies," it seems most likely that these tailors made little beyond "riding-habits and josephs [nightgowns]," as another firm advertised. By the 17th century, the seamstress had elevated herself to *mantua-maker*; the mantua was a loose gown that, for a while, replaced the older-style tailored dress. Dressmaking became a woman's trade, and women would continue making and designing dresses after the mantua had vanished from popularity. A fine dress, like a suit, was close to unique; but this showed in its design more than in precise fitting. The pattern for a gown could only be traced from the gown itself. Society women traded dresses among themselves for copying, with no one but relatives or the closest friends chosen for this mark of esteem.

The "genteel as well as profitable" trade of the mantua-makers was, according once again to the *General Description of all Trades*, "a very expensive one, as well in the Country as in the City." Among women workers, the mantua-maker could indeed rise very high. The "young women apprentices" needed only "a clever Knack of cutting out and fitting, handsome Carriage, and a good set of acquaintance." It seems, though, that the trade may have welcomed most readily young women who had been raised as poor relations in the world of the upper class. They might not have money or position, but they had

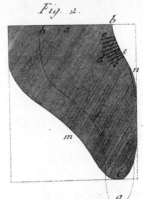

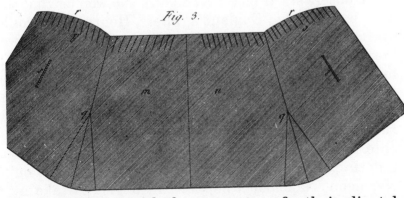

In fashion houses like these, ladies could come to inspect the latest in patterns and designs. (From Diderot's Encyclopedia, *late 18th century)*

been brought up with the proper tone for their clientele. As dispensers of fashion, they had to be fashionable themselves; good looks and deft manners have always helped in this. Female dressmakers generally did not form guilds, while their male counterparts, the tailors, often did.

The *General Description* reported that millinery was "a most genteel business for young ladies." Milliners added innovation after innovation to keep the fashion in dresses from slowing down. A woman who wanted to be noticed decorated herself in a way more novel and imaginative than that of her rival. The skill of the milliner, according to an encyclopedia of the times, "consists principally in...making up and sewing on all the fashionable decorations which she and her client are continually devising." The milliner did not simply sell her trinkets; she thought of new ways to use and arrange them. The French milliners advised their clients on dress and appearance, and on how to compete with their rivals. They became confidantes of the elite, and had a great deal to say about what was and was not fashionable. Milliner Rose Bertin became a friend of Marie Antoinette and one of the first of the *fashion designers*.

The best tailors and dressmakers continued their rise throughout the 19th century. A book published in the 1840s, *The Habits of Good Society*, prescribed for the gentleman a wardrobe of at least one overcoat, one dress coat, one frock coat, four morning coats, five waistcoats, and trousers starting at seven pairs. No wonder that the most successful of England's tailors, Henry Poole, could own a brace of carriage horses admired by the Duke of Portland. Poole began as an apprentice to his father, a military tailor. On inheriting the trade, he moved his shop to Savile Row, a stylish London district formerly inhabited only by surgeons. Poole had made up his mind: He would make his way among the most exclusive of the elite. He had a talent for making friends as well as for tailoring. Poole joined the financial backers of Louis-Napoleon, Napoleon's nephew, in a plot to take over France. Surprisingly, the plot succeeded, and Poole was proud to become Court Tailor of the Second French Empire. There India's rajahs, England's nobles, and Europe's kings came to him for outfitting.

Many other tailors prospered, too, though few expected either Poole's pay or his eminence. Tailoring, as a sound and respectable trade, supported sound and respectable artisans. Robert Lowery, however, never capped his career by a post as Tailor to the King; he became instead one of England's Chartist agitators, an orator for working-class democracy. He had served, at age 10, as a ground worker at a Newcastle mine. He began his tailor's apprenticeship at 14. Lowery was unusual in shifting from master to master until he had completed his apprenticeship in two years; the traditional rules of his guild required six or seven years of apprenticeship.

Lowery never could submit to the regulations of the Newcastle tailors' guild. Its membership provided dues for sickness and burial, a needed service. But, like many of the guilds in their old age, its rule book was used, frankly, to ensure that most business, and most guild funds, went to senior members. If a tailor's shop needed a helper, it sent word to the guild; a name was sent back, selected by seniority. Newcomers could expect no work at all, except during the summer busy season. Senior tailors relied on the power of their guild to ensure a decent living for themselves; others, in the worst case, might have to travel from house to house, looking for clothes that needed mending. Lowery left the trade as a young man. The life of a journalist and political speaker seemed more promising.

Lowery wrote in his *Autobiography* that when his family had chosen tailoring as his career, "It was then very good—wages were high, and it was considered a very respectable employment." He came in for a shock, one not entirely caused by the injustice of his guild. Tailoring had too many journeymen, experienced artisans ready and able to work. As a result, newcomers got very little chance to do the work for which they had trained. Lowery reported: "There was but little chance of regular work for more than six months in the year."

Another blow to the tailor's profession was the practice of *sweating*. Business people set up vast shops, paying their semiskilled workers far below guild standard. What they turned out could be of poor quality, and was

Before the days of factories that made ready-to-wear clothes, many garments were sewn by seamstresses working at home. (Harper's)

made with no particular wearer in mind, but its price would be lower than anything charged by one of the craft's respectable guild members. The tailors' union of London went on strike against the practice in 1834, but the strike failed. "Wages," Lowery wrote at the time, "fell very low, and small masters, as a class, were almost swept away by what may be termed the ready-made clothes manufactories."

He disapproved, of course; but Lowery viewed the scene from the point of view of someone who had hoped to succeed as a tailor. And even someone in his position had

In both East and West, as here in India, large numbers of sewers were employed in one place, to complete large jobs quickly. (Frank Leslie's)

to admit that there had been improvement for tailors' customers, if not for the tailors themselves. "The error of the former system...was, that it allowed nothing between the best clothes with elaborate workmanship, and uncouthly cut and made slops." The factories sold clothing of a third kind; their work became respectable enough in appearance as more skilled tailors were absorbed into the work, but was still sold to customers who could never afford an individually cut suit of "elaborate workmanship."

The poor had always made their own clothing or else bought secondhand garments or the "slops" Lowery mentioned, which were little more than stitched-together rags. Alexander Hamilton, writing in 1791, estimated that in some districts of America four-fifths of the inhabitants made all their clothing at home. The woman of any household beneath the upper crust had to know how to "sew plain." The British as a nation had more money, but a government report found "the poor laboring people in the country towns wearing their own common

TAILORS AND DRESSMAKERS 95

Women only began to dominate the dressmaking trade in the 17th century. (From Tabart's Book of Trades, *1805)*

clothes, principally of coarse homespun linens and woolens."

Tailors could never measure and fit all these people; the people, at any rate, could never afford a tailor. If any clothing was to be sold them, it would have to be made with the customer unseen. Tailors for the poor would stitch according to set patterns and measurements, their work requiring of them nothing but their hands. Accordingly, in the first decades of the 19th century, Robert Lowery and his colleagues found themselves confronted with "ready-made" clothing. Factory-produced suits and dresses would follow a century later.

A mild prosperity gradually emerged in some parts of the working classes. Even near the end of the 18th century, more and more people discovered that they could afford to buy what they had once had to make; the trade in secondhand clothes boomed. Soon tradespeople began to ask: Why not sell new clothing as well? By then, waterpowered mills were producing more cotton and wool than anyone had previously thought possible. Tailors, even outside the factories, labored at a pace they had not known before, often pressing their families into service to expand their output. One American tailor remarked, "A Tailor is nothing without a wife and very often a child." The American army led the way in organizing a mass output of clothes. The United States Army Clothing Establishment set to work at outfitting soldiers for the War of 1812. By 1832, the government reported that the majority of America's tailors kept ready-made clothing in their stores. One tailor in Boston advertised a constant stock of 5,000 to 10,000 items, "every article of apparel to a Gentleman's Wardrobe."

A store of this size could be found in every large American city. These stores made their money, in the words of a characteristic motto, from "Large Sales and Small Profits." Each item might not sell for much, but the retailer could sell its copies over and over again. "Men of moderate income" now made the craft's business, according to one tailor; he advertised "Goods suitable for the millionaire at prices in reach of the millions." The customers responded; they wanted to look like millionaires. Superior clothing was more comfortable than "slops" and lasted longer; it was also a sign of good standing in society. Workers, like anyone else, wanted a share of their society's respect.

At one time, patterns had been handmade, hidden away by any tailor who wanted success. Now money-makers experimented in the mass-production of patterns, arranging them according to general body sizes. One London shop sold nothing but patterns. The handwork of making clothes sped up time and again; measurement of all the new clothing-wearers had to keep pace. From the 1820s to the 1840s, book after book was published, each with a system of instant measurement. One man attempted to make measurement industrial; he patented a measuring machine that wrapped the customer with metal arms, in theory gauging his size more swiftly than

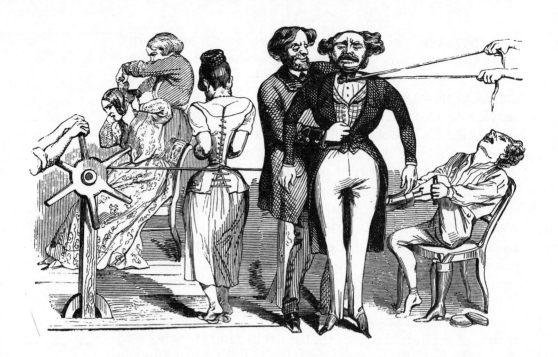

any tailor could. A solution was found at last in proportional measurement. The shape and size of a man's body could be deduced, well enough for his suit to fit him, from just a few measurements. He could memorize these himself and find a matching suit. The production of ready-made clothing became something sure-fire. The customer knew that what he bought for so little would also fit him.

The first ready-made clothes came from the factories. Most of these factories had been set up by a *clothes seller*, with a master tailor in charge. The other tailors had their work divided, with journeymen making patterns, while master tailors cut cloth and pressed finished work. Sewing was still done by hand; to keep up output, more hands were needed than could be fit within a normal workshop. The makings of a suit, including thread, padding, and cut-out segments of cloth, were packaged and sent to seamstresses who worked at home. Sewing the parts together took time but not much skill. The widows or abandoned wives of laborers—women who had once "sewn plain" for their families—now stitched endless bales of waistcoats (vests) to be sent back by messenger for the tailors' inspection.

These seamstresses were an anonymous labor force, managed by the factory's small core of the skilled. The 1832 *Documents Relative to the Manufacturers of the United States* found that Boston tailors had at work 300 men, 100 boys, and 1,300 women. The United States Army Clothing Establishment employed no more than six tailors as cutters, and from 300 to 400 seamstresses.

Men in the industry earned an average of $2 a day, the women and children 50 cents. Apprentices worked their first six months without pay, and sometimes were charged $10 or $15 for learning the trade. Journeymen and seamstresses worked 14 to 16 hours a day. One seamstress said, "I have often sat a whole day and far into the night, making a single shirt."

Henry Mayhew, a London journalist, investigated his city's stores of fashionable ladies' wear, and found small-scale factories hidden behind their walls. *First hands* were the women who cut cloth and waited on customers. The *second hands* supervised all the *third hands* as they sewed, out of sight in their workshops. These women lived in their employer's house, then marched together to work. The shops could turn out great amounts of product rather quickly for a small circle of customers. In sweating, clothes makers had at last found a way to keep fashion from ever slowing down. A society woman could order in late afternoon a gown she would wear at a ball the next evening. A squad of milliners would piece together capes and scarves to complement it.

Milliners at that time made little besides capes and scarves, and some ornaments for bonnets; women of Victorian times preferred their dresses to be the focus of their wardrobes. Styles for all but the most exclusive dresses could be found in such magazines as the new *World of Fashion*, or even, in provincial Dresden, *Dressmaking for Ladies—Universal Pattern Journal*. The customer would choose a pattern, supply the material she wanted, and have the store make up her dress.

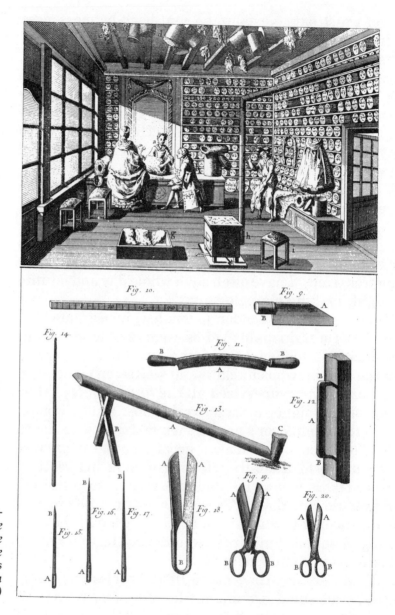

Into modern times, furs continued in high fashion, and the furrier was one of the last fine handworkers in the needle trades. (From Diderot's Encyclopedia, *late 18th century)*

Even with competition from these fashion factories, individual dressmakers with skill could be found everywhere, not just in the large cities but in almost every country town. In America, their work did much to delay mass-production of women's clothes. Wealthy women might patronize certain well-known, talented dressmakers; but women of the lower middle class had their dressmakers too. They could visit a dressmaker's shop employing several seamstresses for fitting and personal attention, as they might go to a beauty salon today. Through the 1920s, a woman of the upper middle class, even without wealth, might still by custom employ one dressmaker for fashionable wear, a second to make lingerie, outfits for the children, and housedresses.

Special gowns could be bought at stores that specialized in these; there a woman could expect to be treated like a lady, with young saleswomen—as attentive and genteel as their mantua-maker forebears—to serve coffee and cake. Gradually such stores introduced a few gowns that had been "part ready-made," yet were attractive and acceptable because of their special quality. By 1910, one could expect to find these in stock as a matter of course. Perhaps the seams had been factory-stitched, but a genuine milliner had devised and sewn on the decorative touches. By World War I, however, women found themselves buying and wearing clothes that no longer had such personal touches. Some women might continue to employ two dressmakers, but many found that a trip to a reputable store selling ready-made clothes could outfit them on a high standard.

In the winter of 1848-49, Lewis and Handford, an American factory, employed 3,672 workers; through these months, the firm claimed to have produced 100,580 items. Sixty years later there was so much mass-produced clothing that one could discover some of it in even the more exclusive women's garment shops. During the half-century between, the new clothing factory owners had labored to double and triple the amount of clothes they could make and sell. New workers flooded in; new machines reduced the skill and time needed to execute their work. While human skills declined, machines were developed that did work of great regularity and precision, such as few humans could ever have matched—quite apart from their speed.

Working these machines in the mid-19th century were

immigrants who had fled from poverty in Europe. They crowded New York City, the chief port of the United States, and factory owners set many of them to work in two industries that needed large numbers of workers: textiles and the making of clothing from textiles. In 1855, two-thirds of the clothing makers in the city had been born abroad; seamstresses, dressmakers, shirtmakers,

Whole immigrant families lugged home piecework to be completed in their cramped, crowded apartments. (By W.A. Rogers, from Harper's Weekly, *April 26, 1890)*

embroiderers, even those who made artificial flowers. Of these foreign-born workers, 66 percent were from Ireland, 14 percent from Germany.

Machines made these workers' tasks simpler and multiplied greatly what they could produce. Even the *cutter*, once an eminent figure, was gradually replaced by a machine. A long blade, hinged on a slotted table, could cut through 18 layers of cloth at one descent. The steam-cutting machine was installed in 1872. The blade rose and fell on its own, at impossible speeds, and the cutter had become merely a holder, extending cloth before the machine, his fingers shielded by tin guards. In 1897, improvements allowed a hundred layers of cloth to be cut at once, the blade following without error the outline chalked on the first. Even so, the cutter was among the most skilled of workers.

For the clothes to be pressed, some way had to be found by which the goose (the special iron used by the tailors) would not cool; each worker could not carry it to the fireplace and then return to the job. To solve this problem, the *pressers* were ordered to stand in columns, while tubes from their irons led to gas or electric generators. With this system, the workers could stand and iron all day; the irons they held would never grow cold. In the early 20th century, pressers were replaced by mechanical arms. A later invention, the *steam-pressing machine*, enclosed the whole process in a metal pod. The pod closed; a weight of wet steam pressed the clothing; the steam was sucked out, and the clothing dried in the vacuum. The workers who operated this machine needed only to press a foot on a pedal, and stand back.

The firm of Douglass and Sherwood installed the first industrial *sewing machine* at its Troy, New York, factory in 1852. Three years later, 172 sewing machines stitched 3,000 of the firm's shirts a day. This device was ideal for ready-made clothing: The number and arrangements of stitches were set in advance and the workers—mostly women—had only to feed the seams smoothly beneath the needle. "It has indeed created our business,"

Douglass and Sherwood proclaimed, in their advertisements' boldest type.

The cutters, pressers, and sewers of the clothing industry worked under, around, and beneath machines. They stood or sat in rows, machines humming, with heads bent and eyes on the machines. The average garment worker of 1884 in New York City earned $6 to $7 a week. The figures in Baltimore were $3.50 to $5. A semiskilled man could earn twice the pay of any woman colleague. The factory work week was officially 60 hours, but often longer.

Conditions at the Triangle Shirtwaist Factory were not at all unusual, though the resulting tragedy was. In 1911, years after the start of union agitation, the workers of the Triangle Factory were still kept locked in until the close of the workday. The factory was shabby, its floorspace not large enough for all the machines the owners had loaded in, let alone for the workers. Paint chips and cloth scraps fell on the factory floor; outside, the fire escape had long since fallen to the ground, where it rested. When a fire broke out at the factory, 154 women died.

The workers of these years—1880 through 1930—were often Eastern European Jews. In 1890, at the start of the influx, representatives of the philanthropic Baron de Hirsch fund counted 111,690 Jewish immigrants in New York City. In all, about two million arrived in the United States between 1880 and 1910, seeking freedom and jobs. Of those who had jobs, 60 percent worked in the garment industry. Employers were clever enough to attract the more skilled hands at low wages by allowing them to stop work on Saturday, the Jewish Sabbath, rather than on the Christians' Sunday.

The work's long hours took discipline, but most immigrants could master its skills readily. Many of the immigrants accumulated a good deal of experience and enough capital—perhaps $50—to open storefront garment factories of their own. Success required working long, tedious hours, but the manager and his helpers could see prosperity and respect waiting just a few years ahead of them—so they worked. They set up in tenement rooms, on tenement rooftops, on fire escapes, along hallways. The manager might use his own apartment as the factory center. These immigrants crowded together, worked where they lived, and worked nonstop. Instead of 60 hours a week with overtime, they worked 84, and then kept on. The pace took its toll, of course; one seamstress named tuberculosis "the tailor's disease."

Three things came of all this work. First, America had the highest-quality and best-selling line of clothes of the early 20th century. David Levinsky, the self-made man of Abraham Cahan's novel *The Rise of David Levinsky*, remarks in a book dated 1915: "The average American woman is the best-dressed average woman in the world, and the Russian Jew has had a good deal to do with making her one." Second, the German Jews, established in America since the middle of the 19th century, were soon being driven from business by shrewd Eastern European

In this great sewing room, hundreds of women hand-sewed the clothes to be sold in Stewart's department store on New York's Broadway. (By J.N. Hyde, from Frank Leslie's, *April 24, 1875)*

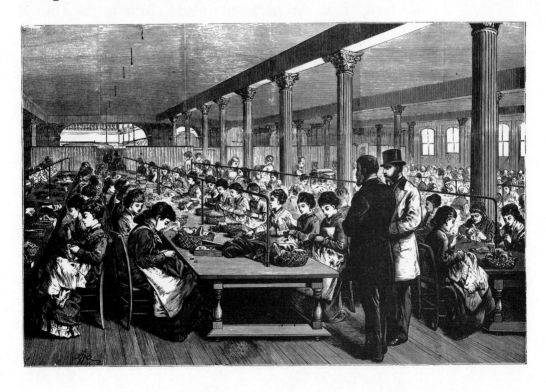

newcomers. New York City's giant garment industry has ever since traced its leadership back to this wave of immigration. Third, those workers who could not see a chance of becoming rich decided that they had been driven far enough.

They founded some of America's most fearless unions, which, after years of fighting, brought results. The International Ladies Garment Workers Union was founded in 1900, with 2,000 members; seven years later, membership had increased to 10,000. Newspapers called July 1910 the "revolt of the cloakmaker"; 55,000 garment workers in New York City went on strike, forcing employers to hire only union members. The fight still goes on.

Apart from factory workers, tailors and seamstresses today are for the most part self-employed. They run small storefront businesses, repairing and making alterations in factory-made clothes.

Of all the needleworkers, *furriers* are the last craftspeople to stitch by hand and make clothing, rather than repair it. All garments made of fur in the United States—whether coats, hats, gloves, or muffs—are made one at a time. Individual workers make almost all the fur clothing made and sold in America. The largest fur company in New York in recent years turned out less than one-half of 1 percent of the American fur trade's product. The rest comes from concerns not much larger than storefront workshops, generally two- or three-person partnerships, where the owners do most of the handwork. Other countries treat fur quite differently, however, using it for factory-made clothing as they would cloth. Denmark's Birger-Christensen plant has 100 employees, for example, while there are rumors of Soviet factories with work forces of up to 9,000.

The Eastern European immigrants who became tailors in New York City also flooded the fur trade. The necessary skills were much the same, though the furriers, unlike the tailors, could command high salaries, even during the Depression of the 1930s. *Shearers* and *sewers* worked with fur, just as they did with tailored clothing.

But it became the fashion for furriers to transform the material they worked upon; this called for skills the tailor never needed. Furriers now include people who dye fur or print new patterns on its surface. This can be quite obvious, as when ink leopard spots are printed on an animal's hide. It can also be very artful. In *feathering*, a turkey feather dipped in ink is used to darken and accentuate a fur's longer fibers. *Pointing* fills in a fur's bare patches with additional hairs. Sometimes these hairs are deliberately chosen not to match; furriers can develop patchwork patterns in the furs they work on.

Customers know that the fur has been altered; but the practice is now respectable, and almost all fur that has been bought, except mink, has been worked on by furriers in this way. The United States government mandates standards for fur bleaching, dyeing, and pointing. The Fur Products Labelling Act, passed in 1951, requires that fur garments contain a label that lists what kinds of fur they are made of. The furrier still has high status among

Though this workroom of the Singer Power Machine Sewing Group may seem crowded, conditions were far better here than in earlier workshops. (By Lewis W. Hine, Records of the Work Projects Administration, #69-RP-56, c. 1937)

the needleworkers, although the trade has been hurt somewhat by animal conservation movements which recommend synthetic furs.

A clothing industry known as *haute couture* (which means "high sewing" in French) has grown up around the practice of preparing new styles of clothing—or fashions—for the public each season. *Fashion designers* conceive of annual "new looks" for clothing. Traditionally, this has meant women's clothing, but almost any sort of personal wear may be marketed with a designer's name on it. Designers are employed by large clothing manufacturers, wholesalers, or the great retail stores. The most successful designers operate as free agents, leasing their services and even founding businesses of their own. Christian Dior went into business for himself in 1947, for example. By 1953, he owned six companies and paid at least 1,000 employees.

The industry has Paris as its center; its first official body, the Syndical Chamber of Paris Couture, was founded in 1868 to guard against raiding of designs and to schedule annual openings, covered by the press, of the designers' new clothes. Since the 1930s, Paris has faced competition from other cities, among them New York, London, Rome, and Tokyo. In 1962, the Council of Fashion Designers of America was founded, elevating American designers to a status equal with the French. By that time, almost all designers were working for the small elite audience that the first designers, 150 years before, had served. Paris, after some resistance, also adopted ready-made clothes, and in 1971 exported over half a billion dollars worth of clothing. In 1975, the Syndical Chamber of French Couture merged with the Syndical Chamber of Ready-to-Wear Couturiers and Fashion Designers.

Fashion buyers represent the stores that must sell what the designers create. Buyers manage departments in large stores and attend the openings of designers' new lines. Most important, they study trade journals, general audience fashion magazines, and the habits of their own

Tailors in private shops had to know not only how to sew but also how to present their work to customers. (Tribute Book)

customers. Relying on experience and intuition, buyers estimate what "look" is coming on in popularity; on the basis of this, the stores place their orders and prepare their advertising. The fashion industry makes an immense amount of money, but the business—forecasting what will next be thought glamorous by the public—is essentially a gamble. It is up to the fashion buyer to see that the people who sell designer clothes make a profit.

Models wear the clothing that the industry wants publicized. Models can be employed by the people who design, manufacture, or sell clothing. Models at the top of their profession display clothes in person at fashion shows, walking up and down a runway, or in photographic sessions for advertisements and fashion magazine features. *Fitting models* appear at closed sessions for buyers. While a photographic model must have unusually good looks, to add glamor to the product, a fitting model's audience is interested primarily in body measurements that are as close as possible to those of the average customer. Fitting models are employees of clothing manufacturers, and may spend part of the year doing light office work.

Photographic and fashion show models lease out their services. Several large agencies represent models, finding them work with important clients in return for 10 to 20 percent of the fees. In 1980, the average annual earnings of full-time models employed by clothing companies was about $22,000. The yearly pay for models kept on contract by the New York City agencies generally ranged from $20,000 to $50,000, with $35,000 as the

The cutter has one of the most important jobs in the garment industry. (From the International Ladies Garment Workers Union's Justice)

average, though an occasional highly successful model can become a millionaire.

In recent decades, clothing factories in industrialized countries have been hard hit by competition from less developed countries, whose poorly paid employees work un-unionized and unprotected in old-fashioned "sweatshop" conditions. Figures from 1969 show that the Far East, endowed with Western machines and cheap labor, led the world in making and selling clothes. Japan exported $451,000,000 worth of clothing; Taiwan, with a population of 14,000,000, exported clothing valued at $295,000,000. But Hong Kong was the biggest exporter of clothes in the Far East. With a total population of only 4,000,000, Hong Kong produced and sold abroad clothing worth $680,000,000. Unionized clothing workers are also losing ground in some industrialized countries, such as the United States, where new immigrants—many of them Asian or Hispanic—are working in old-type nonunion shops.

Independent tailors and dressmakers are rare today, but reasonably well-made clothes are available to most people. A well-dressed customer no longer comes to a tailor for unique clothing, but more generally chooses clothes to match the standard of the clothing worn by everyone around him. In 1959, Nikita Khrushchev, First Secretary of the Soviet Union's Communist Party, met Nelson Rockefeller, Governor of New York State and an heir to one of the greatest private fortunes in history. Khrushchev was a little puzzled about Rockefeller's attire, as he wrote in his memoirs, years later. Rockefeller, he wrote, "certainly wasn't dressed in cheap clothes, but I wouldn't say that he was dressed elegantly either." This man, "not just a capitalist, but the biggest capitalist in the world," was, at a glance, "dressed more or less like other Americans."

Needleworkers have often done work beyond clothes making. Some have specialized in sewing the cloth coverings for furniture and the drapes for windows, for example. From among these *upholsterers* or *drapers* came some of the earliest *interior decorators*. Since drapers provided the great masses of black fabric required for Victorian funerals, some of them also eventually became *undertakers*.

In modern times, most functions in clothes making, upholstery, and drapery have been taken over by factory workers. The relatively few modern needleworkers are generally small shop owners, specializing in the repairing of clothes or the reupholstering of furniture. Some are employed by clothing stores to make minor alterations required by customers; these are most often male tailors, since few women's clothing stores provide such free service.

For related occupations in this volume, *Clothiers*, see the following:
Cloth Finishers
Milliners
Shoemakers and Other Leatherworkers
Weavers

For related occupations in other volumes of the series, see the following:
in *Artists and Artisans*:
Furniture makers
in *Financiers and Traders*:
Merchants and Shopkeepers
in *Helpers and Aides*:
Undertakers

Weavers

The earliest evidence we have of fibers being woven comes from the Swiss Lake Dwellers and is thought to date from about 8250 B.C. Remains of their Stone Age settlements were found in 1853 and 1854, when a very hard, dry winter exposed the bottoms of several Swiss lakes. There archaeologists discovered flax, in various stages of being worked, bits of cloth made of base (a plant fiber), and wool. The tools of these primitive people included *spindle whorls* made of baked clay or stone; these were used as flywheels for spinning wool and flax into thread for baskets, nets, and rough clothing. Crude brushes were also recovered, which the Swiss Lake Dwellers probably used to clean raw wool from the sheep whose bones were found in the silt of these ancient lake homes.

Not until thousands of years later do we have a picture of a *loom* used to weave fibers into cloth. This earliest known depiction of a loom exists on an Egyptian dish crafted around 4400 B.C. The loom is horizontal, has two end bars or beams that stretch the *warp* (the lengthwise yarns), and is pegged to the ground at each of the four corners. The warp is separated by *lease rods* that form a *shed*, that is, an opening through which the weaver could pass the *weft* threads. In this, as in all basic hand looms, the weaver interlaced the weft threads—also called *woof*—at right angles to the warp threads, generally using some device (in modern times, a *shuttle*) to carry the weft threads.

The ancient Egyptian belief in life after death helped to preserve some of these early woven fabrics, which have been found wrapped around mummified bodies. The fabrics had been placed in the tombs to help the dead survive in the next world. All the textiles used for burial were of linen, not wool, because the Egyptians believed that flax—the source of linen fiber—was the cleanest plant, while wool, because it was produced by an animal, was profane. Mummy cloths, often five feet wide and as much as 60 feet long, were made of the finest linen. One such cloth that survives from around 2500 B.C. has 540 warp threads to the inch. Up until the first quarter of the 20th century, the finest linen made by machinery had only 350 warp threads to the inch, and that was considered too delicate to manufacture in large quantities.

Egypt was famous in ancient times for the linen it exported for use in sails. Egyptian flax was supposed to be softer than that from other countries and, as a result, Egyptian linen sails did not wear out as quickly. The Roman historian Pliny wrote in his *Natural History* on the role of flax in sail making:

> How audacious is life that out of so small a seed springs a means of carrying the whole world to and fro, a plant with so slender a stem and rising to such a small height

from the ground when broken and crushed and reduced by force to the softness of wool, afterwards by this ill-treatment attains to the highest pitch of daring.

Early Egyptian looms were horizontal. (In some tomb paintings they appear vertical, but only because Egyptian painters did not use perspective.) The warp—the fibers held stable in the frame—were stretched between two beams staked out by four pegs pounded into the ground. This kind of loom was adjustable in size, depending upon the length of cloth to be woven. When a very long piece of cloth was to be woven, the weavers used roller beams to collect the woven fabric. Around 1500 B.C. the Egyptians switched their looms from horizontal to vertical, propping them up against a wall or fastening them to posts. Instead of the weaver shifting position as cloth was completed, as on the horizontal looms, the weaver could sit comfortably in one place, in front of the vertical loom, moving the cloth as it was woven.

The Roman historian Herodotus was fascinated by Egyptian weaving. "Other nations," he wrote, "in weaving, shoot the woof [the weft, the fibers interlaced into the warp] above; these people put it beneath." He also told of how women leave the weaving to men, at home, while "they are engaged abroad with the business of commerce." In most other countries at this time, women were the weavers, supplying their households with the material needed for clothing. But in Egypt, weaving became a big business. The state-operated linen factories used slave labor, sometimes with conditions approximating the sweatshops of later centuries. The industry was made up of home, public, and temple workshops. Later, during the Roman period, Egypt became the world center for the mass production of linen clothing, especially the tunics that were worn by people throughout the Roman Empire.

Mesopotamia, the ancient region that lay in the triangle of land between the Tigris and Euphrates rivers in

The vertical loom, here set up outdoors, was a perennially popular form; this Iberian weaver is being provided with yarn by the spinner at left. (From The World: Its Cities and People*).*

southwestern Asia, is known as the birthplace of wool, for there sheep were first domesticated. Tablets from the city of Ur, dating from 2000 B.C., shed some light on the early wool industry. These clay tablets, used as account books for the weavers, record huge flocks of sheep, with hundreds shorn in a single day. The tablets also tell of 127 slave girls and 30 children working the wool, and 165 women and girls weaving. Queen Semiramis of Assyria—a romantic figure to whom much progress of that time was attributed—was supposed to have introduced the art of weaving to Mesopotamia. The legend tells that at her death she was turned into a dove and forever after she was worshipped as a goddess.

The great empires that shared Mesopotamia—Assyria and Babylonia—were often at war with each other and with neighboring tribes. Many war captives were brought into the cities and put to work preparing wool and processing it into yarn and cloth. Merchants and kings had workshops where hundreds of slave weavers toiled from dawn to dark. Wool weaving was considered a master craft, and the slave wool workers had a long and difficult apprenticeship. One contract that has survived from this period tells of a cloth master who sent his slave to a five-year apprenticeship to learn wool work. Only the wide variety of colors and designs these ancient people used could justify that amount of time. The apprentice would learn, among other things, the Babylonian custom of dyeing raw wool before spinning it.

Among the slaves brought back to Babylon by King Nebuchadnezzar in 586 B.C. were captive Jews of Jerusalem. In Babylon they learned to make gorgeous textiles, such as those that decorated Nebuchadnezzar's fabulous palace, one of the wonders of the ancient world. The Jews brought these skills back to Jerusalem when they returned to their native land. The earlier Jewish captivity in Egypt had also brought them into contact with linen-making skills. Even before they went to Egypt and Babylon, however, the Jews understood the art of weaving. They wove the hair of goats and camels into materials for tents and the fleece of sheep into wool for clothing. They probably used a few sticks placed horizontally, upon which they stretched yarn that had been spun from sheep's wool, drawing the yarn through by hand.

Delilah may have woven Samson's hair on such a horizontal loom, because the Bible story says she wove her web of hair while Samson slept.

Hebrew legend tells that Ham, Noah's second son, carried on the tradition of weaving. He was supposed to have made all the clothing for the family, having been taught to spin and weave before the Deluge (the great flood). His descendants became wool workers in Canaan and linen workers in Egypt. Jerusalem, in Canaan (now Israel), became an important textile center in ancient times. Many weavers there must have appreciated the quotation from the Bible's story of Job: "My days are swifter than a weaver's shuttle."

According to the Bible, weaving was the work of the Hebrew woman in her home. *Proverbs* 31 describes the virtuous woman as one who "seeketh wool and flax and worketh willingly with her hands. She layeth her hands to the spindle, and her hands hold the distaff [a device used in spinning]. She maketh fine linen and selleth it, and delivereth girdles unto the merchants." The Hebrews generally wore inner garments of linen covered by woolen robes.

Cotton was first cultivated and woven farther east, in ancient India. Some cotton yarn from 3000 B.C. has been found in the ruins of Mohenjo-Daro, a great city in the Indus River valley. Woven samples of cotton from that era have not stood the test of time and weather, however, particularly the hot, humid monsoon climate of the Indian peninsula. Our earliest knowledge of this ancient fabric, therefore, comes only from what was written about it at the time.

Indian cotton first grew on trees; later, shrub varieties were cultivated. The Greek historian Herodotus wrote in 445 B.C. that the Indians "possess a kind of wild plant which instead of fruit produces a wool of a finer better quality than that of sheep, and of this the Indians made their clothes." The Indians wove a plain cotton cloth that they decorated with dyes and paints. When Alexander the Great invaded India in 327 B.C., he was impressed by these printed cottons and brought some back home with him. One of his generals wrote in his journal of the clothing the Indians made out of "linen from trees." He described the Indian clothing as "linen [cotton] garments...a shirt that reached to the middle of the leg, a sheet folded over the shoulders and a turban around the head."

In ancient and medieval India the textile industry was controlled by political power. If a ruler smiled upon the industry, it prospered. If the ruler's attitude was unfavorable, it waned. Rough cloth was made for the masses in rural workshops. Cloth for royalty, the wealthy, and for export was made in state workshops. Only the finest weavers were allowed to work on the ritual hangings for the temples. The *Arthasastra*, a handbook of administration from the third century B.C., tells of strict rules for the textile industry and describes methods for distributing materials to spinners and weavers. Although women were not allowed to hold jobs in this period, exceptions were made and weaving was permitted by widows and retired *prostitutes*, most of whom worked at home.

Even farther east, silk was the dominant fiber for cloth. Chinese legend credits the discovery of silk to the Empress Si-ling-chi, wife of the great prince Huang-ti. About 2700 B.C., so the legend goes, the empress chanced to watch a small caterpillar wrapping itself in a cocoon; she looked around and found other caterpillars doing the same. One of the cocoons fell into her tea, the story continues, and when she took it out, she found that she could unravel the cocoon into a long strand that was strong and lustrous. Si-ling-chi was venerated in China as the goddess of silk. She is also given credit for making the first loom, although it is likely that some kind of loom was in use before then. A day in Si-ling-chi's honor was celebrated in China until as recently as 1911.

The province of Shantung in China was the cradle of silk weaving. The Chinese introduced the weaving of patterned textiles to the world. Their tradition states

This Asian weaver, using a horizontal loom, is being supplied yarn by the spinner at right, with a form of spinning wheel. (From The Pictorial Sunday Book)

that they built the first *drawloom* in 1298 B.C. A drawloom is a loom with a system of cords the weaver can use to lift different strands of the warp, in order to weave complicated repeating patterns. It took other civilizations many centuries to approach the weaving technology of the Chinese. Silk was worn by all classes in China. It was an important commodity in and of itself. It was hoarded, used as a medium of exchange, and used to pay tribute and taxes. Often silk paid as taxes was in the form of spun threads, which were then woven into cloth by artisans employed in imperial workshops. The size and style of the final product varied with the fashion of the time, in later centuries, especially, with the desires of Western buyers.

The Chinese kept their knowledge of silk a secret for thousands of years, although raw and woven silks were exported from China all over the ancient world. Imperial decree threatened death by torture to anyone who tried to pass the secret to others. Silk cloth was so common in China that Chinese aristocrats sometimes preferred clothes of cotton gauze imported from India to all but the finest silks.

The Chinese released their secret of silk to their neighbors, the Japanese, in the second century A.D. by sending them silkworm eggs. Chinese and Korean weavers emigrated to Japan in the fourth and fifth centuries A.D. The skill of these weavers was so valuable to the Japanese that they were given land and titles.

But the truth about sericulture (silk cultivation) reached the West only in the sixth century A.D. when the Byzantine Emperor Justinian bribed two monks to smuggle silkworm eggs and seeds of the mulberry tree on which they fed, hidden in hollow bamboo canes, across Asia to Constantinople. Silk weaving as an industry had been established centuries earlier in Near Eastern cities such as Alexandria, Antioch, and Jerusalem, but weavers had been obliged to use silk imported, at great price, from China.

The art of weaving was celebrated in myth and legend by the Greeks and Romans. In ancient Greece, Athena was revered as the goddess of weaving. The Roman poet Ovid, in his *Metamorphoses,* told the story of the beautiful maiden Arachne who dared challenge Athena, pitting her skill in weaving against that of the goddess. This so enraged Athena—Greek gods and goddesses never appreciated challenges from mere mortals—that she changed Arachne into a spider, that skilled weaver of the animal world. Scientists today classify spiders as belonging to the class *arachnid.* The Romans saw weaving as a metaphor for fate. The word *cloth* is derived from the name Clotho. Clotho was one of the three Fates of Roman mythology, who wove the fabric of human destiny. The other two Fates were Lachesis, who spun the thread of life, and Atropos, who cut the thread and thus brought life to its end.

Greek weavers would set up their looms at the various temples. Each of the Greek gods had separate temples and was worshipped at a special season. The weavers would stand their upright looms in front of the temple whose god was being celebrated and weave cloth for new robes for the god. Sometimes extra cloth would be sold in

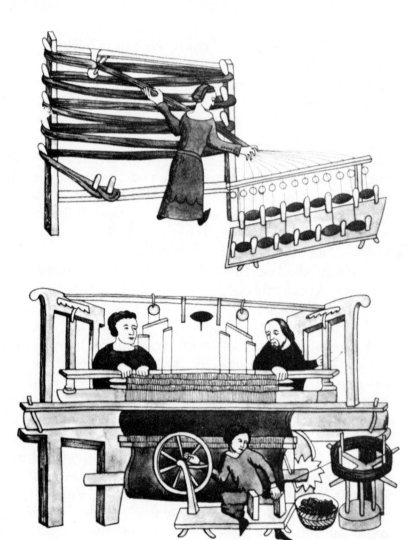

Weaving was often a communal or family affair; here a woman is arranging the warp and a child is spinning, while two men are weaving. (Archives Communales, Ypres, Belgium)

order to raise funds for the temple or the priests who attended it.

Weaving in Greece and Rome was primarily a household industry, however, done in the home to produce clothing for family members. The loom was a common household object. Weaving was most often the woman's responsibility, from the poorest home to the richest, especially in Greece, where women were encouraged to be busy. Penelope, in Homer's *Odyssey*, bent industriously over her loom, weaving a shroud for her father-in-law, Laertes. She put off the suitors who clamored to marry her (while her husband Odysseus was missing and presumed dead after the Trojan War) by saying that she would not consider their offers until she had finished the shroud. Each night the faithful wife would unravel that day's work, extending the task in the hope that her husband would return, which he eventually did.

Even the legendary beauty, Helen, after she and her lover, Paris, had run away to Troy, directed the maidens of her household in spinning and weaving woolen cloth for clothing. In Rome, the Emperor Augustus made a point of wearing clothing from wool spun and woven at home.

The Romans themselves had little interest in weaving. In the early ages of Rome, it was the Etruscans, from northwest Italy, who supplied Rome with woven cloth. The tunic, the classic Roman costume, was merely an adaptation of Etruscan dress from about 800 B.C. An important cloth-weaving center near Rome was Sybaris, a colony in southern Italy that had been founded by the Greeks in 650 B.C. Sybaris was ruled by a matriarchy (a government in which power was passed down through the woman's side of a family) and concentrated on the quality of cloth that it wove.

Both the Greeks and Romans wore garments made primarily from wool. In both areas sheep-raising was an important industry. In Greece, linen was considered suitable only for women; flax was raised, but the linen industry was concentrated more in its colonies than in Greece itself. The Romans built agricultural "colleges" where experiments with improved methods of flax and wool production took place.

Silk was the fabric that the Romans most admired. They first saw it in their opponents' banners at the Battle of Carrhae in 53 B.C. Caesar brought it to Rome in 45 B.C. for use in his canopies. The Senate attempted to ban or at least restrict it in the first century A.D. as an expensive luxury, but—like prohibitions on other products through the ages—the ban on silk only increased people's desire for it. As the Roman Empire spread, trade increased with the East, and the Romans became the greatest consumers of silk in the Western world. The silk-weaving centers of Alexandria, Antioch, and Jerusalem were well situated for trade with the luxury-loving Romans. Although at first silk was worn only by wealthy Roman women, it soon became the favorite garb of men as well. The mad Emperor Caligula was reprimanded for dressing like a woman in silks. Dress became so elaborate that more laws were passed in an effort to control the spread of luxuries the government considered wasteful.

Silk weaving prospered while Rome flourished, but declined sharply in the West after the fall of Rome in the fifth century A.D. In the Dark Ages that followed, Western Europe suffered a breakdown of society, and weavers generally retreated to the monasteries, those traditional medieval havens. However, the eastern reaches of the Roman Empire continued to revel in power and wealth. The Byzantine Empire, as these parts became known, expanded greatly under the Emperor Justinian (527-564). His court was lavish and luxurious, fed and clothed by imports from the Near and Far East.

The Near Eastern weavers of the Middle Ages were masters of design and materials. Fabrics surviving from that era provide evidence of weavers' intelligence and devotion to their art. Elaborate textiles were used not only in the lavish clothing worn at court but also in the vestments of priests and the tapestries and other decorations of churches as well as of homes and palaces. The rituals of Christian burial required woven shrouds and rich people were buried in elaborate silk winding sheets. The court at Constantinople (the ancient capital city of Byzantium, renamed by the Emperor Constantine in 330 A.D.) had its own silk-weaving workshops. These workshops supplied the court with the sophisticated woven silk textiles that are now preserved in the treasuries of the great cathedrals of Europe. Because large numbers of women were employed in them, these workshops were called *gynaecea* (from the Greek word for woman).

The Byzantine emperors held a virtual monopoly on silk weaving in the West from the fourth to eleventh centuries A.D. Their imperial workshops, where workers employed the highest quality raw materials to craft shimmering textiles, attracted experienced weavers from all over the world. Craftspeople traveled to Constantinople for the opportunity to work with the finest materials and share in the prestige of the court. These were closed shops, however. The number of laws punishing runaway workers or those who would employ them suggests that it was easier to get into a *gynaeceum* than to leave one. The first of these Byzantine workshops was set up at Constantinople; later others were established in a few honored cities, such as Alexandria.

There were also private textile workshops, for the imperial workshops supplied only the court and the churches. But private workshops were hampered by the unavailability (and poor quality) of the raw materials needed for the making of cloth. The Emperor Justinian regulated the price of silk; his wife, the Empress Theodora, entrusted a favorite with control of the silk trade. The result was that the price of silk skyrocketed far above the emperor's controls, thus wiping out the private workshops dealing in silk. Many of the silk weavers fled to Persia where silk—imported from the East or, later, made locally—was available to them. In the Byzantine Empire, only the imperial weavers were then able to work with silk.

A collection of trade ordinances, the *Book of the Prefect*, has survived from 10th-century Constantinople. The prefect was the highest-ranking city official, the representative of the emperor in dealing with trade groups. There were five silk guilds in 10th century Constantinople: the merchants, dealers in Syrian silk, dealers in raw silk, spinners, and weavers. The industry was strictly regulated. The prefect had a staff that

After the West learned the techniques of sericulture from China, silk spinning and weaving was carried on in many workshops in southern Europe. (Biblioteca Ambrosiana, Milan, 14th century)

carefully inspected the workers as well as the finished product. Those who disobeyed any of the many rules were dealt with severely. Someone caught dyeing raw silk with murex (the famous *royal purple* dye of the Phoenicians) had his hand cut off. Anyone caught selling silk to a Hebrew was flogged. Anyone selling materials to strangers without permission of the prefect had his goods impounded.

The expertise of the Byzantine weavers and their ability to create elaborately patterned textiles was prized throughout Europe and the Near East. When Constantinople was taken by the Turks in 1453, those weavers who had not fled to the Christian kingdoms of the West were taken into Turkish weaving workshops. Constantinople became an Islamic center, eventually renamed Istanbul.

While the Byzantine Empire was expanding on the northeastern shore of the Mediterranean Sea, another empire was spreading with lightning swiftness to conquer the southern and western shores. In 636, only four years after the death of their prophet, Mohammed, the Moslems conquered Syria; five years later they captured Alexandria. By the late seventh century they occupied all of Northern Africa, and by the early eighth century, Spain. Reacting to the decline and fall of the Roman Empire, Mohammed had warned his people away from the love of luxury, stating in the Koran, the Moslem holy book, that "only those who have no part in the future life clothe themselves with silk."

The teachings of the Prophet also stipulated that there would be no pictorial representation in painting, textiles, or any other medium, of any living thing. Reconciling the teachings of the Prophet with their newly acquired wealth led the Moslems to a new style of art and design. The consensus was that their religion forbade the creating of luxurious materials but did not prohibit the wearing of them. Their spoils of war included not only lavish textiles but also Christian weavers who, as their slaves, could use their exquisite skills to create new patterns more in keeping with the work of the Prophet.

Like the Byzantine emperors, the Moslem *caliphs* (princes) established their own textile workshops. The *tiraz* (palace workshop) was a symbol of prestige; a prince displayed his wealth in the number and output of his weavers. The work was often identified by an inscription naming the *tiraz* where the textile had been woven. The weavers were most often Christian slaves from the countries that the Moslems had captured. Their most famous products were colorful patterned rugs, which could be breathtakingly beautiful. The Arab writer Makrizi reported "carpets embroidered with gold and silver" in Cairo's royal palace. Persia's Shah Rohk, who ruled through the first half of the 15th century, banned the making of rugs and carpets outside the royal workshops. Sheep were raised for high-grade wool, and

Many weavers in northern Europe specialized in making linen clothing and covers, while others became skilled tapestry weavers. (By Jost Amman, from The Book of Trades, *late 16th century)*

the carpets' weavers and designers could be elevated to court posts.

Carpet makers wove a loose foundation of yarn on their looms. Then they strung strands of dyed wool through the warp and weft, knotting one end of each strand, while allowing the free end to stand out above the foundation. The strands had to be knotted one at a time, and their arrangement atop the woven warp and weft constituted the craft's real work. Once a row of strands had been knotted, the carpetmaker brushed it with a weighty comb; this pressed one row of knots against the one below, concealing the woven yarn underneath. The wool's tufted free ends rose above the carpet's surface of knots; they were cut to a uniform height.

In 827 the Moslems conquered Sicily. Although only a small Mediterranean island at the tip of Italy's boot, Sicily had long been prized by imperial conquerors. It had belonged to Greece, Carthage, Rome, and the Byzantine

The techniques of carpetmaking, raised to a fine art in Asia, became widespread in Europe as well in modern times. (From Diderot's Encyclopedia, *late 18th century)*

Empire, in turn. The Moslems endowed it with a gift that would assure its fame and future: They established a silk-weaving industry, setting up looms for the weavers who had followed their conquering armies. The growth of Sicily as a weaving center attracted foreign weavers from Persia, Syria, Constantinople, and India, each bringing new ideas for textures and designs.

When the Normans conquered Sicily and took it from the Moslems in 1072, they did not destroy the weaving trade; in fact, Roger II, the Norman king, expanded it. He imported expert weavers, by force, from Greece, and set up his own *tiraz* in his royal palace in Palermo. There the Greek weavers worked side by side with the Islamic-influenced Sicilian ones. The fabrics these weavers turned out became renowned throughout the world, especially for their use of gold. A traveler to Sicily around 1189 wrote:

I must not pass in silence over those workshops in which silk is spun in strands of different colors which are blended by various methods of weaving (one, two, three, and six threads at a time)...There, too, are many other ornaments of different kinds and colors, in which gold is woven into the silk and the variety is set off by the sparkle of precious stones.

The king took pride in the output of his royal workshops; he had workers weave into the borders of this precious cloth the name of the workshop and the date of the weaving.

At the end of the 12th century Sicily was taken over by the Germans. Although trade and the arts declined after this, the Germans did use the expertise of the weavers and embroiderers of the *tiraz* in Palermo. They created the coronation vestments used by the Holy Roman Emperors. These priceless robes, lavishly embroidered with gold, pearls, and other jewels, are banded with woven strips inscribed in Latin and Arabic and bearing the date of their weaving computed according to the Moslem calendar. They were worn by the ruling emperors until 1794. The French conquest of Sicily in 1266 finally ruined the textile industry there. Many Sicilian weavers fled the turmoil and escaped to Italy.

In the 13th century the land we now call Italy was a group of small states, usually at war with one another. When the fighting stopped, these states were often involved in trading that was greatly stimulated both by their nearness to the Mediterranean, where goods from throughout Europe and Asia were traded, and by the Crusades and the pilgrimages of Christians visiting the holy places of their religion.

The town of Lucca in Tuscany in the ninth and tenth centuries became a stopover for rich Christian pilgrims who were traveling to Rome. Rich pilgrims appreciated fine fabrics, and Lucca became a weaving center turning out fabrics of linen and wool. In the 12th and 13th centuries, when materials from Asia became easier to obtain, Lucca's weavers became known for their fine damask (rich patterned fabrics named after Damascus, a city long associated with the style), as well as exquisite cloths of gold and intricate brocades (fabrics with raised designs) depicting religious subjects. The weavers who had fled from Sicily added Byzantine and Islamic touches to the Luccese style with fanciful animals and waving bands with Arabic writing. Early in the 14th century, however, Lucca underwent political turmoil. Many talented weavers fled to the other great cities of Italy, notably Florence, Venice, and Genoa, making them textile centers.

By the 14th century, Florence was a prosperous and thriving city, perhaps the greatest city of all Italy. It was almost completely controlled by guilds, associations of merchants and artisans known in ancient Rome as *collegia*. These associations, although professional in purpose, were also social and political. One member of a Florentine cloth maker's guild was the founder of the powerful Medici family. As patrons of the arts, this family brought Florence into its golden age in the 15th century. There were two groups of guilds in Florence, as in many other guild cities of Europe: the guilds of the merchants and the guilds of the artisans. Florence's two great cloth guilds were the *Calimala*, composed of workers in unfinished cloth that was imported from all over Europe, and the *Arte della Lana*, the guild of the cloth manufacturers.

The merchant guilds were usually formed first and held the greatest power. They most often won this power by gaining charters from the rulers and controlling trading rights. Much of the merchant guild's power derived from their reserves of capital (money), which were needed to finance the cloth-making industry. Merchants had the capital to purchase the raw materials the workers needed and to buy back the finished cloth by the piece. They could, and did, monopolize the industry, setting prices and controlling the import and export of raw materials and goods.

The craft guilds were smaller and, at least at first, not as powerful as the merchant guilds. Each guild served a specialized occupation, including silk reelers, silk weavers, dyers of *fast* (permanent) colors, dyers of *fugitive* colors (those that tended to fade or run), and wool weavers, among others. A guild was made up of masters, journeymen, and apprentices. Strict rules were made concerning the teaching period, called the *apprenticeship*, required to master the trade—its length, the skills, and even the sequence of skills to be learned by the apprentice. Craft guilds also acted as a quality control service, with members of the guild inspecting finished products in order to maintain the high standards on which they based their professional pride.

As the craft guilds grew in strength in Florence—to 30,000 workers in the cloth-makers' guilds by 1350—they came to resent the monopolistic pressures of the merchants' guilds. The merchants, wielding greater political power than the artisans, actually made laws forbidding the craft workers to organize. Throughout the 14th century in Florence there were revolts of craft workers against the merchants. The merchants, in time, prevailed, but the craft guilds were able to form legally and grow in strength.

In earlier centuries, weaving in Florence had been dominated by the work done in monasteries, where weavers had fled when Rome fell. The guilds helped bring weaving out of the monasteries and develop it as an industry. Early Florentine weavers worked with wool and linen. Silk was introduced in the 13th century, giving the weavers greater opportunity for artistic expression in fabrics that could demand higher prices. By 1470 Florence was known throughout Europe as the leader in silk weaving. That fame was to last for a relatively short period, until 1530, when the city was besieged by the forces of Pope Clement VIII.

Many of the weavers who had fled Lucca in the early 14th century then left Florence and traveled to Venice, an important seaport on the Adriatic Sea. Venice was historically, as well as geographically, close to the Byzantine Empire. The Crusades brought increased wealth to the city, for Venice controlled the main sea route of the Crusaders and other pilgrims to the Holy Land. Marco Polo's return to Venice in 1295 increased the interest of Venetians in Chinese crafts, especially fabrics.

The Venetian weavers, centered as they were on the trade routes from Europe to the East, became familiar with all fibers and all weaves. No fabric was too difficult for them to make or match. They were particularly known for their skill in weaving velvets. In 1347 a guild of velvet weavers was established in Venice. In 1421 two different classes of velvet weavers were registered, those who could weave only plain velvets and those who wove patterned fabrics. In the 14th century, Venice had over 17,000 woolen cloth weavers, who imported their wool from Spain as well as England. The Venetian predominance in textiles waned later with the loss of its sea power. World trade supremacy was taken over by the Portuguese, the Dutch, and the English when a short sea route to India was discovered in the late 15th century.

The fourth great Italian textile center was Genoa, a seaport on the western edge of Italy. Because of internal strife, Genoa did not reach its prominence as a weaving center until the 15th and 16th centuries. Genoa was well known for the patterned velvets its weavers created. On velvet and some other plush fabrics loops of yarn formed the thick surface called a *pile*. In Genoese velvets the pile was cut at two different heights to form a pattern; this gave them a rich quality that was unlike the fabrics of other cities.

One of Genoa's former cloth weavers brought a different fame to the city: Christopher Columbus, born in Genoa to a family of local cloth weavers. Entering weaving as an apprentice at the age of 12, he was still working as a wool weaver (along with his father) as late as 1472. But his dreams were elsewhere. He saved his money and, in 1473, bought an interest in a local wool company. He began his sailing career as a buyer of raw wool and seller of finished woolen cloth. His sailing led to the discoveries that would help transfer world power from the nations that surrounded the Mediterranean to those that faced the broad Atlantic.

Meanwhile, weaving had been reviving in Northern Europe. As early as Roman times there were tribes skilled in spinning and weaving in Flanders, a region of Northern Europe in what is today Belgium, between the Somme and Moselle rivers. The inhabitants of this area, the Flemings, were named for their skill, for *fleming* means *weaver*. During the Dark Ages this craft was kept alive in the monasteries in the area. Cloistered monks spun and wove fabrics of wool, at first just for their own use but later, as volume grew, to be sold or bartered to the people in the countryside around them.

In the ninth century Flemish cities began their rise as textile centers. Cities such as Ghent, Ypres, Bruges, Douai, and Brussels became known for the intensity of their industrial life as well as the products of their looms. The cities were like giant factories, in which almost everyone was involved in textile production. Bells would ring throughout the city at the start of the workday, at the beginning and end of the midday break of one and a half hours, and at the close of the workday. The length of a working day was rigidly set by town authorities: eight hours in winter and 13 hours in summer, or as long as there was daylight. The Sabbath was kept sacred and there was no work on Saturday afternoons. In addition many holy days were celebrated on which work was prohibited.

Weavers were considered a high class of artisans. They usually worked on their own premises and often owned their own looms, although some weavers employed others to work for them. The Flemish cities imported weavers from other areas who were attracted by the opportunities for work and the growing reputation of the quality of the Flemish textiles.

Specialization in Northern Europe's cloth industry first became a strong trend in Flanders during the 12th

The clothes may be different, but the styles of weaving and spinning have changed very little from earlier times in this 17th century illustration. (Authors' archives)

century. Weaving became an occupation distinct from spinning. This specialization in tasks grew into a greater concern for quality. The Flemish fabrics became luxury fabrics, expensive but worth the price to the wealthy throughout Europe. Cheap cloth was always made in rural areas for family needs but the well-made fabrics of Flanders were symbols of quality weaving throughout the world. These fabrics proudly displayed the seal of the city in which they were woven and often a distinctive mark that identified the individual weaver as well.

A bitter rivalry grew between city and rural weavers in Flanders in the late Middle Ages. The rural weavers had begun to take the market away from their city rivals; they used cheaper wool from Spain so that they could charge lower prices. The city-trained cloth weavers sneered at the rural weavers because their fabrics could not compare to city-woven stuffs. They even sent out armed men to the rural weaving areas to burn looms and wool. Sporadic incidents broke out between rural and city cloth makers during the 14th and 15th centuries. But it was religious persecution that effectively broke up the Flemish cloth industries in the 16th-century, driving Protestant textile

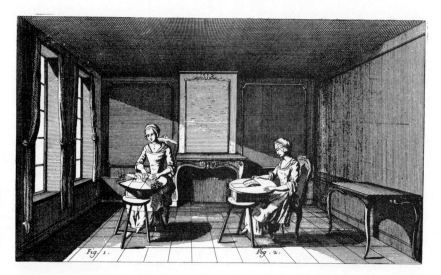

Lacemaking was often done on a small scale in the home and required considerable dexterity and skill. (From Diderot's Encyclopedia, *late 18th century)*

workers out of Flanders into northern Ireland, France, and England.

Lace making, later to be a chief industry of the Netherlands, developed at some time before the 16th century. It is handwork, not strictly weaving with a loom, but *lace makers* originally stitched their patterns on a woven cloth called a *ground*, as *embroiderers* do. Gradually the ground threads were dispensed with and the lace pattern was made directly. Needlepoint laces developed when lace makers arranged linen threads in patterns on paper, then built up a structure of further threads on top. This structure is called a *cordonnet*. Together, the foundation and *cordonnet* can make web-like patterns of great intricacy.

Tapestry weavers were also important in this period. The first known guild of European tapestry weavers was formed in Paris in 1254. Through the Dark Ages, most tapestries--wall coverings decorated with patterns and scenes--had been woven in the monasteries. Tapestry workshops spread through France, the Netherlands, and the British Isles during the 14th and 15th centuries. Many of these workshops employed no more than one weaver and an apprentice. Some tapestry makers followed noble patrons on their travels, becoming nomad weavers.

At the Gobelins factory in France, fine tapestries were made for the royal family. (From Diderot's Encyclopedia, *late 18th century)*

A tapestry was not woven with a single set of weft threads running along its entire width; instead, each segment of its pattern was determined by a weft of its own. The weft threads were colored, and made up the picture that the weaver composed. Like carpetmakers, tapestry weavers brushed their work with a heavy comb. The weft threads bunched together to hide the undyed warp threads.

Weavers worked with *painters* in devising tapestries. The medieval weaver was expected to reproduce whatever the painter demanded, working from the artist's sketches, called *cartoons.* Tapestries often came in sets, their number depending on how many walls had to be covered. By the 17th century, Charles Le Brun, at the command of his royal patron, could conceive of a "Life of Louis XIV," composed of 14 separate tapestries.

During the early Middle Ages, England had been a great source of supply for the raw wool used by Flemish weavers in making their fine woolen cloth. But English weavers were not as adept at creating those woolens themselves. English weaving in the early Middle Ages was more of a cottage and monastery industry, where simple fabrics were woven for home and church use. Beginning in the early 14th century and becoming especially strong during the Elizabethan era, English rulers in various ways encouraged the development of a domestic English cloth industry.

King Edward III was considered "the Father of English Commerce." In the 14th century, he encouraged Flemish cloth weavers to immigrate to England and teach their weaving techniques to the English. "Our people who are ignorant of the weaving art," the king is supposed to have said, "as knowing no more what to do with their wool than do the sheep that wear it, and as to any artificial drapery, their best cloth being no better than coarseness, for want of skill in this weaving." The immigrant weavers were settled in various places throughout England and were soon instructing English cloth workers. The Hundred Years War, which began in 1336, added to the flow of Flemish immigrants to England. The war had stopped the export of English wool to Flanders, causing starving hordes of once-proud Flemish weavers to rove the countryside begging bread because there were no raw materials with which to work.

Not all the English were happy about the influx of foreign weaving talent. In London, where the weavers had the oldest chartered craft guild, the foreigners were not allowed into the established guilds but were forced to set up their own, although holding to the same rules as the English guild of weavers. The Flemish weavers were unfriendly with immigrants from Brabant (a region that today lies partly in Belgium and partly in the Netherlands). The two groups had to be assigned separate churchyards to be linked to their guilds: St. Lawrence Pountney for the Flemish and St. Mary Somerset for the Brabanters.

In the English cities, as in Flanders and in Italy, the craft guilds were strong social, moral, and religious, as well as professional, influences. As on the Continent, the craft guilds grew up in England after and in response to pressures from the powerful merchants' guilds. The latter had been formed by financiers and business owners who had money and influence to control the cloth industry and those who worked at the crafts of which it was composed. The craft guilds were formed as a protection against the merchants, who held the capital and monopolized the supply of raw materials, as well as having influence with the king. Skilled cloth workers such as weavers joined with others of their own craft. Membership was compulsory, even for the women who practiced the craft. (Many other guilds at the time excluded women.) Chaucer's Wife of Bath--"of cloothmaking she hadde swich an haunt, / She passed hem of Ypres and of Gaunt"--could have belonged to such a weavers' or cloth makers' guild. Winchester, Lincoln, Oxford, Nottingham, and Huntingdon had weavers' guilds that were famous and important.

As on the Continent, English guilds controlled the training of their members by an apprenticeship system. Novices, usually children of 12 to 14 years of age, were chosen by a master to train for a specified number of years, generally seven. The *novice*, or *apprentice*, would live in the master's house, usually being treated like one of the family, and would work each day (except, of course, for Sunday and holy days) from 4 a.m. to 7 p.m. On completing the apprenticeship, a novice became a *yeoman*, or *journeyman*, and was free to seek employment elsewhere or even travel from place to place learning new techniques.

Weavers were often individual craftspeople working out of their own homes. A typical rural or small-town weaver might live and work in his own two-story cottage.

Most weavers were also farmers, growing their own vegetables, and possibly planting a field of oats or barley to provide extra income. A weaver's loom was placed on the upper floor where he could work when bad weather prevented him from farming. A weaver could make a salable length of cloth by working continuously for a few days. When he had finished it, he took it to market, sold it, and bought raw wool for his next project. Typically the weaver's wife and children would transform the raw wool into the yarn needed to work the loom. Four to six spinners were required to supply each weaver.

By the early 14th century the demand for rural cloth production increased to such an extent that more and more homes became workshops, the farmers leaving their agricultural tasks behind them. Some skilled weavers, nevertheless, took to the roads when they could not find steady employment in their own home towns. They would go from town to town weaving yarn that had been prepared by the local householders. Traveling weavers could not carry their own looms with them; they had to use looms in the homes of strangers. Some of these weavers settled in the growing towns that were becoming textile centers.

Ownership of the looms was an important economic consideration. Most weavers at this time owned their own looms, a tradition that dated from Anglo-Saxon times when the *geloma* (loom) was a common domestic tool; the word *heirloom* shares its roots with this Anglo-Saxon word. The modern economic system of capitalism involves ownership of the means of production by wealthy owners (*capitalists*) rather than by workers. The seeds of capitalism were sown in England in 1339, when Sir Thomas Blanket bought and set up his own looms for weavers in their homes. Blanket's immortality lies less in his role as an early English capitalist, however, than in the articles produced on those looms, which were named after him.

The *cottage system* of textile manufacturing gradually gave way to the *domestic system*, in which the raw materials were owned by a class of employers called *clothiers*, who farmed them out to spinners and weavers. A household would work together to produce the finished products; the women, children, and old people would often prepare the yarn by spinning and carding, while the fathers and sons would generally do the weaving. The clothiers bought back the finished work from the households, paying by the piece. The guilds would supervise the quality of the finished materials. In 1360 the wages of English weavers were fixed by Parliament, but in the late 16th-century Parliament authorized the local Justices of the Peace to set the wages of weavers and spinsters.

In England the monarch and Parliament were much involved in the textile industry. One example of intervention was their official encouragement of weavers to emigrate from Flanders. During the 16th-century reign of Elizabeth I thousands of Dutch and Flemish weavers fled the ravages of the Duke of Alba, who destroyed the city of Antwerp. English rulers also made laws that forbade the import of foreign cloth and the wearing of anything but English fabrics. In 1555 the Weavers' Act of Parliament forbade rural clothiers to keep more than one

Sometimes a whole family would work together to complete a process, as here, weaving a decorative fringe. (From Diderot's Encyclopedia, *late 18th century)*

loom supplied with raw materials for production. This law--applying only to rural workshops, not city ones-- showed the power of the craft guilds as well as the weavers' fear of the next, seemingly natural, step in the development of cloth production, the *factory system*.

English weavers were most hesitant about anything that would take their work out of their homes and put it under the supervision of others. Indeed, they did not welcome any real change in their industry. For example, although the power of running water could have eased the toil of English weavers as it had for those on the Continent, laws were passed prohibiting the use of water mills to provide power for spinning and weaving. In 1485 the owner of a woolen factory who had installed a water mill was attacked for his innovation. Inventors would not design equipment for spinners and weavers because of their strong resistance to any change that would jeopardize the tradition of spinning and weaving as part-time occupations at home. This strong opposition kept the factory system of cloth making from growing in England until machinery was finally introduced that was too expensive and too large to be used at home.

Meanwhile a substantial weaving industry had developed in France. France's involvement in the woolen textile industry dates back at least as far as Charlemagne, who in the eighth century A.D. established textile markets at Lyon and Rouen and also organized spinning schools on his estates. The French became known more as silk weavers than as wool weavers, however, largely because of the religious persecution that took place in France in the 17th century. When the Edict of Nantes, a decree that had granted Protestants political equality, was revoked in 1685, Huguenot (Protestant) textile workers, who worked primarily with wool, fled to England, northern Ireland, and Scotland, effectively destroying the French woolen industry.

King Louis XI had introduced silk weaving to the French city of Lyon, in the last half of the 15th century, by encouraging silk weavers from the Italian town of Lucca

Aristocratic visitors often came to view the great tapestry works called the Gobelins. (From Diderot's Encyclopedia, *late 18th century)*

to settle in Lyon. Some moved to Tours in 1470, where they taught the delicate and elaborate techniques of silk weaving to the French. In the early 16th century King Francis I brought to France the Renaissance in art and culture that was flourishing in the Italian city states. He promoted Lyon as a silk-weaving center by importing Italian silk weavers to train the French, and allowing Genoese and Lucchese weavers to set up weaving schools in 1538. The immigrants were exempted from all taxes, providing that they agreed to settle in Lyon for the rest of their lives.

The Renaissance took firm root in France, appealing strongly to the lavish courts of the French kings. King Henry IV was particularly interested in the silk industry because he felt a great sense of competition with the Italians and wanted to outdo them in order to exclude their luxurious silken products from France. He bettered the living and working conditions of the silk weavers he housed within the Louvre, since the 12th century a royal fort and palace. By the end of his reign in the early 17th century, the weaving of silk had become one of France's greatest industries; there were over 12,000 looms in Lyon alone.

The silk industry flourished in France. Given the constant shortage of labor, abandoned children were almost always apprenticed to the silk trade. In families, the tasks involved in making silk were shared. The women unwound the silk cocoons, sometimes even carrying them around in their bodices to keep them warm until ready to hatch, and spun and rolled the thread from the cocoons onto spools. The children took care of the small tasks involved in silk work. The men did the weaving. Professional regulations of the Fabrique de Lyon, the silk guild founded in 1545, forbade women to work as the more highly paid loom operators. The silk industry grew steadily. Fashions changed swiftly and often, creating occasional immense demands for the luxurious fabric. But fashions could change for other reasons, especially in periods of official mourning and of revolution. In 1789, the year of the French Revolution, there were 20,000 unemployed silk workers in Lyon.

Across the ocean, in the Americas, weaving had been developed centuries before the Europeans arrived. Traditionally it was thought that twining, a method of making yarn which is a preliminary step in the development of weaving, began in Peru around 2500 B.C. But evidence now indicates that weaving was known there almost as early as 6000 B.C.

Surviving textiles in Peru, which were found preserved in dry burial grounds, show a development in

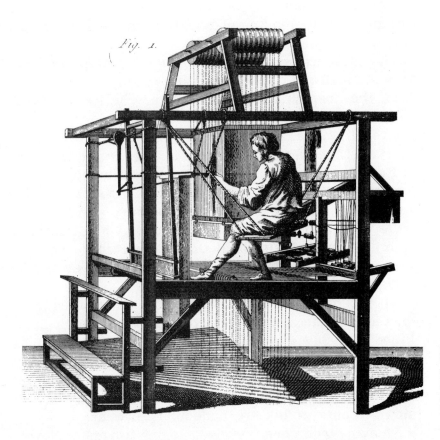

Fig. 1.

Lace, as well as ribbons and braid, was produced commercially on looms, although homework continued. (From Diderot's Encyclopedia, *late 18th century)*

culture and at the same time in methods of weaving. The Inca culture, which lasted just over a century (1438-1530), placed a high value on textiles and their production. The most beautifully woven textiles were made by young women known as Virgins of the Sun. Chosen for their ability by Inca officials, they were sequestered in temples to ply their craft in service of the Sun and other Inca gods. Inca costumes were simple in style but could be elaborate in color and pattern, to signify rank or place of origin. Weaving was a full-time occupation for many Incas, male as well as female. Indeed, lengths of cloth were used to pay taxes and tributes.

Textile production did not stop when the Incas were conquered by the Spanish in the 1530s. The Spanish made use of the native weaving talent by setting up weaving workshops. They influenced weaving style and brought in new weaving materials, such as sheep's wool, linen, and silk.

The influence of the Spanish conquest on the Aztec culture in Mexico in the 16th century was more destructive than the Spanish influence in Peru. The Aztec city of Tenochtitlán (now Mexico City) was a civilized metropolitan area of nearly one million people, with great markets that specialized in fine textiles. As in the Inca culture, lengths of cloth were used as money. One's wardrobe indicated one's station in life, with the wealthy wearing highly decorated fine textiles. The Aztecs believed that the goddess Xochiquetzal had invented spinning and weaving and that she watched over the women who wove on their backstrap looms, working in designs based on their religion.

Xochiquetzal must have wept when the Spanish conquered the Aztecs in the early 16th century. The Spanish killed or enslaved most Indian nobles and imposed their European culture upon those who were left. They shunned the fine Aztec textiles, preferring imports from Europe or the Far East. The Aztec traditions in weaving survived only as folk art made for local wear.

Weaving techniques survived among two major Native American groups in the North American Southwest: the Pueblos and the Navajos. The Pueblos were a tribe which flourished from about 700 A.D., building the large stone and adobe living complexes whose ruins bear their name. They were a peaceful people who lived harmoniously in these enormous, multistoried buildings, which sometimes contained over 100 rooms. Pueblo weaving techniques were highly advanced, especially during the middle period of their culture, from 1100 to 1300 A.D. For some reason as yet unknown, their culture broke up after this period, and they abandoned their pueblos in the northern cliffs of New Mexico to migrate to the valley of the Rio Grande. There the Spanish found them when Coronado and his men arrived in 1540. When the Spaniards arrived in full force, they taxed, enslaved, and tortured the Pueblos, although the establishment of Christian missions in the area did preserve and protect some of their culture. Weaving workshops were set up in some of the missions, where the baptized Native Americans could create the 33 inches of cloth per family that the Spanish demanded as tax.

Many Pueblos fled from the Spanish north to Navajo country. The Navajos were a more warlike people, and the Spanish kept out of their territory. It was around 1680 that the Pueblos introduced the Navajos to the weaving techniques that would make the Navajos famous in the 19th and 20th centuries. Navajo legend, however, credits the Spider Woman with teaching women how to weave on a loom that the Spider Man told the men how to make.

Weaving was an important part of a Navajo woman's life, and knowing how to weave gave her prestige. Unmarried women were not allowed to sit at the loom. There were special ceremonies dealing with weaving, including one for overwork. Men would sometimes weave, too, using the smaller belt looms rather than the large rug looms in front of which the women sat. Navajo blankets were famous for their warmth and durability, especially among the American soldiers who took possession of New Mexico in 1846. One soldier wrote, "It seems anomalous to me that a nation living in such miserably constructed mud lodges should, at the same time, be capable of making, probably, the best blankets in the world."

Weaving in the Colonies that were to become the United States was largely a cottage industry. As has been true in many parts of the world, throughout history, families worked together in their own homes to produce the materials they needed to clothe themselves and supply their households. The New World attracted weavers and other textile workers from many nations of Europe. The Puritans from England settled in New England, many Irish textile workers went to New Hampshire, the Dutch weavers went to New Amsterdam (later to become New York), and Mennonite weavers settled in

Pennsylvania. Colonial fabrics were matched to the Colonial style of living—plain and functional.

The Colonies had a mercantile (trading) relationship with England. The Colonies provided the motherland with food and raw materials and, in return, England sold them finished goods, such as textiles, furniture, books, and other luxury items. As the settlements grew into towns and cities there was more potential for textile industry in the Colonies but England discouraged such activity by laws and other means, in order to protect its own thriving textile industry. The heavy-handed strictures of such English laws as the Wool Act of 1699, which forbade the export of American wool and woven cloth, rankled the independent spirit of the settlers and helped lead to the American Revolution.

The Revolution and the War of 1812 first interrupted and then snapped the ties to the Old World. Self-sufficiency in textile production became a priority for the new nation. George Washington set up a weaving house at Mount Vernon where weaving was done for 25 neighboring families. In 1817 the United States Congress passed a general tariff act to protect the fledgling American textile manufacturers, imposing duties (taxes) on imported cotton, woolen, and linen cloth as well as other manufactured goods.

What changed the whole weaving industry was the onset of the Industrial Revolution, starting in England. In the late 17th and early 18th centuries England began to change from an agricultural to an industrial economy. The textile industry was, after agriculture, the second largest in England at this time, and it grew as the number of farmers decreased. For a while textile production remained largely a cottage industry. The cottagers would retire to their looms or spinning wheels when the weather was not right for farming or when a piece of cloth was needed.

One invention that simplified the work of the weaver at this time was the *flying shuttle*. The width of a piece of cloth had always been limited by the span of a weaver's outstretched arms, because the shuttle was passed from hand to hand. The problem was partially solved by putting two weavers side by side at a broadloom and having one weaver pass the shuttle to another. Then in 1733 John Kay, a Lancashire *clockmaker*, put the shuttle on wheels and added to the loom a hammer to hit the shuttle in order to push it through the warp. This flying shuttle enabled the weaver who sat at the loom and pulled strings attached to the hammer to make cloth wider and faster. The weaver's speed was sometimes double or even tripled, up to 20 yards a day. But the flying shuttle did not really catch on until the 1760s, partly because the spinners who supplied the weavers had had difficulty keeping up the supply even before the flying shuttle was invented.

Thus the inventors who sought to improve the machinery used in textile production first sought to

Even before industrialization had fairly started, weavers' shops could be crowded, unattractive places. (By William Hogarth, British Museum, 18th century)

speed up the spinning of yarn rather than the weaving of cloth. Three inventions changed the textile industry irrevocably, bringing it into the age of machinery: the *spinning jenny*, a machine for spinning multiple strands of yarn at once, invented by James Hargreaves in 1767; Richard Arkwright's *water frame*, invented (or copied) around 1768; and Samuel Crompton's *spinning mule*, an even better yarn-making machine with up to 1,000 or more spindles, invented in 1799. Because these machines were much larger than the simple home-spinning implements they replaced, the spinning part of the textile process was moved into mills or factories. The production of yarn increased immensely. Weavers were so busy keeping up with the supply of factory-spun yarn that many gave up their agricultural tasks to devote all their time to weaving. Some moved from their rural cottages into the towns to be closer to the spinning mills and the clothiers who bought the woven cloth.

This became the golden age of weaving. Weavers could afford to live and dress like gentlemen. Gilbert French, in his biography of Samuel Crompton, inventor of the spinning mule, describes the flamboyant style of these weavers when things were going well:

They brought home their work in top boots and ruffled shirts, carried a cane, and in some instances took a coach. Many weavers at that time used to walk about the streets with a five pound Bank of England note spread out under their hat-bands; they would smoke none but long 'churchwarden' pipes, and objected to the intrusion of any other handicraftsmen into the particular rooms in the public houses which they frequented.

But the golden age of weavers was a short one. In 1787 Edmund Cartwright, a clergyman-poet, invented a loom that could be operated by horsepower, waterpower, or the recently invented steam engine. Although Cartwright went bankrupt, others made improvements on his inventions and, by the 1820s, the *power loom* was in common use. There was much opposition to the power loom among weavers. Informally organized with the legendary Ned Ludd as the ringleader, some weavers—known as Luddites—rioted and attacked factories, smashing machines. One group that was especially active in the Luddite riots of 1811 and 1812 was the framework knitters of the lace industry. In 1812 Parliament sided, not surprisingly, with the machine and factory owners, by passing a Framework Act that increased the penalties on people found guilty of machine wrecking.

The deeply entrenched opposition of the weavers to the power loom helped shift the focus of the English textile industry, which in turn changed the world's fashions, from wool to cotton. The wool weavers had a long history of guild membership, the cozy cottage system, and other traditions that militated against their acceptance of machinery and the factory system. But cotton was a fairly new textile in England, and the workers in the industry were therefore more open to innovation. Cotton was also better suited than wool to the high speed of the power looms because of its strength and lightness, and it was available in abundant supply from the United States.

The cotton mills employed women and children in preference to men, not only because they were a source of cheap labor but also because they adapted more easily to the discipline of the factories. Factory discipline, after all, was alien to these people, few of whom had a clock in the house. A factory, especially when compared to one's own home, was like a prison, in which one could not smoke, drink, eat, or sleep when one wanted.

The factory system caused a breakdown in the family, and therefore in the social structure, at this time. In the past, a family had worked together to produce a piece of cloth in the home, traditionally the women spinning, the children helping out, and the men weaving. The factory, however, demanded a different kind of organization. The machine imposed its speed upon the worker rather than the other way around. The work was constant and did not allow any interludes of child care or farming, much less gossip or socializing. People were no longer able to work in their own homes. Women and children found work in the mills more readily than the men, causing an uncomfortable situation in which women and children were working while men were unemployed.

The handloom weavers, who out of artistic and traditional pride chose to continue at their cottage looms—those workers who had once proudly displayed five pound notes in their hats—were forced to work longer hours for a mere fraction of what they had previously earned. A Parliamentary committee study, published in 1835, reported that:

A very great number of the weavers are unable to provide for themselves and their families a sufficiency of food of the plainest and cheapest kind; that they are clothed in rags...that notwithstanding their want, they have full employment; that their labour is excessive, not infrequently sixteen hours a day.

During the second half of the 18th century the British Parliament had forbidden the export of textile machinery (as well as plans or models of them) to the North American Colonies. The British even tried to prevent trained operators from emigrating. But the secrets spread and, in 1790, Samuel Slater, a skilled mechanic who had worked for Arkwright in England, set up a factory to spin cotton in Pawtucket, Rhode Island. In 1814, the power loom, that threat to the independence of the English handloom weaver, was brought to Waltham, Massachusetts, by Francis C. Lowell. The Industrial Revolution had begun in the United States.

Handloom weaving continued to be practiced in the growing United States during the early 19th century, mainly in the home. There were fewer looms than spinning wheels, because several people in the family would work on the same loom. The drafts that showed weaving patterns were treasured and often passed down to succeeding generations within a family. The loom might be in a separate house, as on George Washington's plantation, or perhaps in a loft, in the colder climate of New England. Some weavers traveled from town to town, often long distances on the frontier, weaving on local householders' looms, using yarn that the householders had spun themselves.

But machine-made cloth took over, as it had in England. American factory owners learned, or tried to learn, from the mistakes of the British, attempting to set up their factories in ways that would not disrupt the family structure and destroy the social fabric. One way they did this was to hire young unmarried women to run the machines and mills. These mill girls, called *operatives*, worked long hours in airless factory rooms, and the houses they lived in had strict rules of conduct. Yet the mill girls enjoyed their independence from the drudgery of housework and farmwork, and the opportunities for additional education that the mills offered. Harriet Robinson, a young woman employed at a textile mill in Lowell, Massachusetts, gives a view of what the life was like:

The discipline our work brought us was of great value. We were obliged to be in the mill just such a minute, in every hour, in order to doff our full bobbins and replace them with empty ones. We went to our meals and returned at the same hour every day. We worked and played at regular intervals, and thus our hands became deft, our fingers nimble, our feet swift, and we were taught daily habits of regularity and of industry; it was, in fact, a sort of manual training or industrial school. Some of us were fond of reading, and we read all the books we could borrow. One of my mother's boarders, a farmer's daughter from the state of Maine, had come to Lowell to work for the express purpose of getting books, usually novels, to read, that she could not find in her nature place...I had been to school quite constantly until I was nearly eleven years of age, and then, after going into the mill, I went to some of the evening schools that had been established, and which were always well filled with those who desired to improve their scant education, or to supplement what they had learned in the village school or academy.

One related craft in which some individual work has survived is knitting. *Knitters* use needles to hook together strands of wool, silk, cotton, and other materials. Knitting with two needles turns out flat pieces of fabric; four needles are needed for tube-shaped pieces, such as stockings. The techniques of knitting have been known since Egyptian times, but hand knitting did not become popular until the 14th and 15th centuries, when it came into general use in many parts of Northern Europe, especially in Scotland and England. William Lee invented the first *knitting machine*, using two needles, in 1589; but it was not widely employed until the mid-18th century. By the 19th century four-needle machines had been developed, and knitting became increasingly a factory operation.

Hand knitting is still a popular pastime. Knitting, by hand or with the help of simple machines, is also one of the few remaining cottage industries in the United States and Northern Europe. People, most of them women, knit clothing at home, sending their work for payment to the clothing firms, some of which provide them with patterns. The employer does not have to deal with unions, and may take advantage of that fact. Some hand knitters are terribly underpaid; one claimed that she worked 35 hours a week for $50. Others in more affluent areas, such as the skiing regions of northern New England, can earn perhaps four times as much by knitting at home for ski-wear firms.

For the most part, the craft of the independent weaver has been swallowed up by mills throughout the world, the work being overseen by relatively unskilled *factory*

While most weaving is now done in factories, handwork continues in certain areas, often with many in the community involved, as were these Wensley Dale knitters. (Engraving after G. Walker, from Costume of Yorkshire, 1814)

workers. Handloom weaving could never match the speed of mass production by machinery. However, hand weaving does still exist as a folk art in various areas of the world. During the 19th and early 20th centuries traders encouraged Navajo women weavers to produce work in new styles, introducing them to new materials and design ideas, and acting as their marketing agents. This weaving with an eye to the tourist market, especially after the railroad came through in the 1880s, cheapened the woven rugs and blankets with coarse yarns and garish artificial colors. However, craft revival among the weavers, begun in the 1920s, restored the natural colors and yarns and encouraged the Navajo weavers to return to the high quality of weaving that shows their artistry. The same pattern had been seen in many parts of the world where folk-weaving appeals to affluent buyers. Handwoven textiles are prized today almost as artifacts, pieces that remind us of a world long gone, when men and women, not machines, wove the cloth so central to their lives.

For related occupations in this volume, *Clothiers*, see the following:

Cloth Finishers
Fiber Workers
Spinners

For related occupations in other volumes of the series, see the following:

in *Artists and Artisans*:
Clockmakers
Painters
in *Harvesters*:
Farmers
in *Financiers and Traders*:
Merchants and Shopkeepers
Bankers and Financiers
in *Manufacturers and Miners*:
Factory Workers
in *Scholars and Priests*:
Monks and Nuns
in *Warriors and Adventurers*:
Prostitutes

Suggestions for Further Reading

For further information about the occupations in this family you may wish to consult the books below.

General

Baxandall, Rosalyn, Linda Gordon, and Susan Reverby, eds. *America's Working Women: A Documentary History 1600 to the Present* (New York: Vintage, 1976). A collection of articles, with clear editorial notes.

Brereton, F.S. *Clothing: An Account of Its Types and Manufacture* (London: B.T. Batsford, 1931). Although outdated and somewhat eccentric, this British book provides historical background on clothing manufacture.

Cambridge University Press. *Cambridge Economic History of Europe*, Volume 2: *Trade and Industry in the Middle Ages* (Cambridge, England: Cambridge University Press, 1952). A scholarly work, very helpful in defining job tasks.

Cassiday, Doris, and Bruce Cassiday. *Fashion Industry Careers* (New York: Franklin Watts, 1977). Focuses on current careers, especially designer and model.

Dolber, Roslyn. *Opportunities in Fashion* (Skokie, Illinois: JGM Career Horizons, 1980). Describes current occupations with some history, mostly American.

Foner, Philip S. *The Factory Girls: A Collection of Writings on Life and Struggles in the New England Factories of the 1840's by the Factory Girls Themselves and the Story, in Their Own Words, of the First Trade Unions of Women Workers in the United States* (Urbana, Illinois: 1977).

Foner, Philip. *Women and the American Labor Movement*, in two vols. Vol. 1: *From Colonial Times to the Eve of World War I*, (1979), Vol. 2: *From World War I to the Present* (1980) (New York: The Free Press).

Hardy, Jack. *The Clothing Workers* (New York: International Publishers Co., 1935). Prepared by the Labor Research Association.

Kennedy, Susan Estabrook. *If All We Did Was to Weep at Home: A History of White Working-Class Women in America* (Bloomington and London: Midland, 1979).

Lane, Peter. *The Industrial Revolution: The Birth of the Modern Age* (New York: Barnes & Noble, 1978). A well-written history that adds a social perspective to the economic changes taking place in this era.

Levine, Louis (Lewis Lorwin). *The Women's Garment Workers* (New York: B.W. Huebsch, 1924).

Power, Eileen, and M. Poston. *Medieval Women* (Cambridge: Cambridge University Press, 1975). Delightfully written, full of insight; includes beautifully selected illustrations showing medieval women in a variety of occupations.

Power, Eileen. *The Wool Trade in English Medieval History* (London: Oxford University Press, 1941).

Riis, Jacob A. *How the Other Half Lives: Studies Among the Tenements of New York* (New York: Scribner's, 1890). A clear and moving study of conditions among immigrants in New York City in 1890.

Rooke, Patrick. *The Industrial Revolution* (New York: John Day, 1971). A Young Historian's Book; helpful for an overall picture of the process of industrialization in Britain and the United States.

Salzman, Louis F. *English Industries of the Middle Ages*, revised edition. (Oxford: Oxford University Press, 1924).

Seidman, Joel. *The Needle Trades* (New York: Farrar & Rinehart, 1942). A very good portrayal of rising industrialization and unionization in the United States.

Stockham, Peter, ed. *Little Book of Early American Crafts and Trades* (New York: Dover, 1976). Unabridged republication of Part I of the work as published by Jacob Johnson in Whitehall (Philadelphia) and Richmond in 1807 under the title, *The Book of Trades or Library of the Useful Arts*.

Unwin, George. *The Guilds and Companies of London*, fourth edition. (New York: Barnes & Noble, 1964). The development of guilds and companies from the days of Henry Plantagenet to those of Victoria.

Ware, Norman J. *The Industrial Worker, 1840-1860* (Boston: Houghton Mifflin, 1924).

Wymer, Norman. *English Town Crafts* (London: Batsford, 1949). Covers many of the clothing crafts in an entertaining, anecdotal style.

Milliners and Hatters

Amphlett, Hilda. *Hats: A History of Fashion in Headgear* (Chalfont St. Giles, Buckinghamshire: Richard Sadler, 1974). Mainly on fashions but includes some useful information on the making of men's hats.

Fisher, Leonard. *The Hatters* (New York: Franklin Watts, 1965). One of his series of books on "Colonial American Craftsmen"; includes a step-by-step description of a felt hatter's work.

Giaferri, Paul-Louis de. *Millinery in the Fashion History of the World* (New York: Illustrated Millinery Co., 1928).

Hat Trade Publishing Co. *How Hats Are Made* (New York: Hat Trade Publishing Co., n.d.). Factory work step-by-step, *circa* 1920s.

Holmes, R.A. *From Hare to Hair* (New York: Crofut & Knapp 1932). A promotional pamphlet describing the work of a Crofut & Knapp hat-making factory.

Weiss, Harry B., and Grace M. Weiss. *The Early Hatters of New Jersey* (Trenton, New Jersey: New Jersey Agricultural Society, 1961). Documents on the early 19th-century hat factories and hatters.

Shoemakers and Other Leatherworkers

Burford, Alison. *Craftsmen in Greek and Roman Society* (Ithaca, New York: Cornell University Press, 1972).

Cambridge University Press. *Cambridge Economic History of Europe*, Volume 6: *The Industrial Revolution and After* (Cambridge: Cambridge University Press, 1965). Provides figures on English and American machine production of shoes in the late 19th century.

Campion, Sam S. *Delightful History of the Gentle Craft: An Illustrated History of Feet Costume* (Northampton, England: Taylor, 1876). A curious combination: a survey of shoes through the ages, a history of the shoemaker, a defense of the trade, and a collection of poems, epigrams, and anecdotes on the subject.

Dobbs, Brian. *The Last Shall Be First: The Colourful Story of John Lobb the St. James's Bootmaker* (London: Hamish Hamilton, 1972). An anecdotal account of a fashionable bootmaker's firm, with a useful chapter on the artisans and their techniques.

Fisher, Leonard. *The Shoemakers* (New York: Franklin Watts, 1967). One of his series of "Colonial American Craftsmen"; includes a step-by-step description of an 18th-century shoemaker's work.

Wilson, Eunice. *A History of Shoe Fashions: A Study of Shoe Design in Relation to Costume for Shoe Designers, Pattern Cutters, Manufacturers, Fashion Students and Dress Designers, etc.* (New York: Theatre Arts Books, 1968). Fashions throughout England's history, with many illustrations.

Tailors and Dressmakers

Ghurye, G.S. *Indian Costume* (New York: Humanities Press, 1967).

Houston, M.G. and F.S. Hornblower. *Ancient Egyptian, Assyrian and Persian Costume* (London: A. & C. Black, 1920). Plates of clothing, with explanatory captions.

Howe, Irving. *World of Our Fathers* (New York: Simon and Schuster, 1976). A cultural history of Eastern European Jews in America; vivid on the garment industry in New York City's Lower East Side.

Judelle, Beatrice. *The Fashion Buyer's Job* (New York: Merchandising Division, National Retail Merchants Association, 1971).

Kaplan, David G. *World of Furs* (New York: Fairchild Publications, 1974). The operation and present circumstances of the fur industry, specifically in America.

Kidwell, Claudia B. *Suiting Everyone: The Democratization of Clothing in America* (Washington, D.C.: The Smithsonian Institution Press, 1974). A valuable social history of clothing's industrial revolution; first-rate information, with many plates.

Lambert, Eleanor. *World of Fashion: People, Places, Resources* (New York and London: R.R. Bowker, 1976). A directory to each nation's fashion traditions, designers, industry councils, and training schools.

Lowery, Robert. *Robert Lowery: Radical and Chartist*, Brian Harrison and Patricia Hollis, eds. (London: Europa Publications, 1979). The autobiography of a British tailor who left the trade for political agitation; tells of guild rules and the condition of the craft in the first third of the 19th century.

Waugh, Norah. *The Cut of Men's Clothes 1600-1900* (New York: Theatre Arts Books, 1964).

Waugh, Norah. *The Cut of Women's Clothes: 1600-1930* (New York: Theatre Arts Books, 1968). For each century, gives the types of clothing worn, changing tailors' practices, typical patterns, and quotations from writers of the day; well illustrated.

Wilcox, R. Turner. *The Mode in Furs* (New York: Scribner's, 1951). Western fashions in wearing furs, from ancient times to the 1950s; includes a chapter on how fur and skins are prepared.

Weavers, Spinners, Cloth Finishers, and Fiber Workers

Adrosko, Rita J. *Natural Dyes and Home Dyeing.* (New York: Dover, 1971).

Boulnois, Luce. *The Silk Road* (New York: Dutton, 1966). Translated by Dennis Chamberlin. A fascinating history of silk—its trade, uses, power, the nations it influenced.

Caplin, Jessie F. *Knitting: Its Products and Processes* (New York: Dry Goods Economist, 1927).

Dilley, Arthur Urbane. *Oriental Rugs and Carpets* (Philadelphia: Lippincott, 1956).

Haarer, A.E. *Ropes and Rope-Making* (London: Oxford University Press, 1950). On factory processes.

Krochmal, Arnold and Connie Krochmal. *The Complete Illustrated Book of Dyes from Natural Sources* (Garden City, New York: Doubleday, 1974). Mainly a craft book with recipes for natural dyes; includes a section on the history of dyestuffs.

Leggett, William F. *The Story of Wool.* (Brooklyn, N.Y.: Chemical Publishing, 1947). An excellent history of the growing, weaving, and merchandising of wool the world over.

Lewis, Ethel. *The Romance of Textiles* (New York: Macmillan, 1937).

Plymouth Cordage Co. *The Story of Rope.* (North Plymouth, Mass.: Plymouth Cordage Co., 1928).

Powys, Martan. *Lace and Lace-Making.* (Boston: Charles T. Branford, 1953).

Shook, Anna. *The Book of Weaving* (New York: John Day, 1928). Mainly about the craft of weaving; includes a short history.

Thompson, F.P. *Tapestry: Mirror of History* (New York: Crown, 1980).

Wilson, Kax. *A History of Textiles* (Boulder, Colorado: Westview Press, 1979). An excellent history, beautifully illustrated, with international coverage and extensive bibliographies.

INDEX